A Ripple of Hope

A Ripple of Hope
The Life of Robert F. Kennedy

Barbara Harrison and Daniel Terris

LODESTAR BOOKS
Dutton   New York

Library of Congress Cataloging-in-Publication Data

Harrison, Barbara,
    A ripple of hope: the life of Robert F. Kennedy / by Barbara Harrison and
Daniel Terris.
        p.   cm.
    Includes bibliographical references and index.
    Summary: A photo essay that focuses on the life of Robert F. Kennedy, from
his childhood with the Kennedy clan to his assassination in 1968, with an
emphasis on his commitment to social issues.
    ISBN 0-525-67506-X (alk. paper)
    1. Kennedy, Robert F., 1925–1968—Juvenile literature.   2. Kennedy,
Robert F., 1925–1968—Pictorial works—Juvenile literature.   3. Legislators—
United States—Biography—Juvenile literature.   4. United States. Congress.
Senate—Biography—Juvenile literature.   [1. Kennedy, Robert F., 1925–1968.
2. Legislators.]   I. Terris, Daniel.   II. Title.
E840.8.K4H37   1997
973.922′092
[B]—DC20   96-42447   CIP   AC

Published in the United States by Lodestar Books,
an affiliate of Dutton Children's Books,
a division of Penguin Books USA Inc.,
375 Hudson Street, New York, New York 10014

Published simultaneously in Canada
by McClelland & Stewart, Toronto

Editor: Virginia Buckley   Designer: Dick Granald

Printed in the U.S.A.
First Edition
10 9 8 7 6 5 4 3 2 1

The lights begin to twinkle from the rocks;
The long day wanes; the slow moon climbs; the deep
Moans round with many voices. Come, my friends,
'Tis not too late to seek a newer world.
Push off, and sitting well in order smite
The sounding furrows; for my purpose holds
To sail beyond the sunset, and the baths
Of all the western stars, until I die.
It may be that the gulfs will wash us down;
It may be we shall touch the Happy Isles,
And see the great Achilles, whom we knew.
Though much is taken, much abides; and though
We are not now that strength which in old days
Moved earth and heaven, that which we are, we are—
One equal temper of heroic hearts,
Made weak by time and fate, but strong in will
To strive, to seek, to find, and not to yield.

From "Ulysses"
by Alfred, Lord Tennyson

Each time a man stands up for an ideal, or acts to improve the lot of others, or strikes out against injustice, he sends forth a tiny ripple of hope, and crossing each other from a million different centers of energy and daring, those ripples build a current which can sweep down the mightiest walls of oppression and resistance.

Robert F. Kennedy
Cape Town, South Africa
1966

Contents

Bobby Kennedy speaks with a young girl in Bakersfield, California. GEORGE BALLIS

The Mississippi Delta
(1967)

In April 1967, Robert F. Kennedy was a United States senator from the state of New York. His father had given him a million dollars when he turned twenty-one. He lived with his wife, Ethel, and their ten children on a five-acre estate called Hickory Hill, just outside of Washington, D.C.

Bobby Kennedy's brother had been president of the United States. As attorney general in John Kennedy's administration, Bobby was known as the number-two man. Now, in 1967, Bobby Kennedy was thinking about running for the highest office in the land.

So why was he here in sharecropper country, a thousand miles from the corridors of power on Wall Street and Capitol Hill?

In the tiny hamlet of Cleveland, Mississippi, Bobby Kennedy visited a run-down shack. The stench in the windowless room was fetid, and the senator struggled against nausea. A small girl, barely walking age, was pushing rice kernels around on the floor. The youthful senator knelt next to her. She was about the same age as his own son Matthew.

He gently spoke to her. "Hello . . . hi . . . hi, baby," he said. The child's

1

stomach was bloated and distended by hunger. Her face was expressionless. She did not look up. A few feet from the child, a misshapen mattress was propped up on bricks, and cockroaches scampered across the splintered floor.

A thin shaft of light shone on the child from the open door. What did the future hold for this child? Bobby brooded. The United States was the richest nation on earth, but millions of Americans still did not have enough to eat. From urban ghettos in Northern cities to this forsaken corner of Mississippi, millions of children were suffering.

Bobby Kennedy did not need to visit the Mississippi Delta. He did not need to look into the desolate face of a child whose eyes held so little hope. He could have been at the Hickory Hill swimming pool, or playing touch football with his children, or at a fund-raiser with wealthy donors for his next campaign.

But the fires of outrage burned in Bobby Kennedy's soul. He could not rest easy while hunger, poverty, and hopelessness ravaged children anywhere in the United States.

"Our lives on this planet are too short and the work to be done too great," Senator Kennedy said, "to let the violence of hate, despair, and indifference dominate the land."

His own life was cut tragically short by an assassin's bullet, but no man of his time was more passionate in his quest for a nation where children could grow up free from hunger and fear.

chapter one

The Seventh Child
(1925–1952)

*I will drink
Life to the lees.*[1]

In autumn, off the rocky coast of New England, briny lobstermen lift their harvest from the sea while inland, near white-steepled churches, tireless farmers reap squash and giant pumpkins. By Thanksgiving, trees that only days before were ablaze with bright golds and vermilions are bare.

In this place of hills and promontories, Robert Francis Kennedy's ancestors established a foothold, and it is here that Bobby was born in the family home in Brookline, Massachusetts, on November 20, 1925.

He was Rose (Fitzgerald) and Joseph P. Kennedy's seventh child. That, in itself, was a lucky omen, but he was also the third son. The day was a bright one, with lots of sunlight pouring through the bedroom window to help Dr. Frederic Good in the baby's delivery.

Bobby was a boy after four girls—Rosemary, age seven, Kathleen, six, Eunice, four, and Pat, one. "He's stuck by himself in a bunch of girls," his grandmother Josie Hannon Fitzgerald worried. "He'll be a sissy."

Joe Sr. and Rose Kennedy on their wedding day BOSTON GLOBE

His oldest sibling, Joe Jr., was ten years old and in the fifth grade. His brother John, called Jack, was eight years old and in the third grade.

Bobby's ancestors were Irish. The Fitzgerald family had come to America from western Ireland in the County Limerick village of Bruff. The Kennedys' homestead was in County Wexford in Duganstown. The families came to America between 1846 and 1855, where they worked as peddlers, coopers, and laborers in East Boston.

Bobby's two grandfathers, John "Honey Fitz" Fitzgerald and Patrick "PJ" Kennedy, became active in Boston politics. Rose Kennedy once said, "My babies were rocked to political lullabies."[2]

His grandfather Fitzgerald once served as mayor of Boston. He was a bubbly, good-natured man who sang "Sweet Adeline" at the drop of a hat and had an instinct for the underdog.

His grandfather Kennedy ran a tavern and served as a ward boss. He curled his mustache at the tips. He was a calm, quiet man, not nearly so flamboyant as Honey Fitz. Grandfather Kennedy shared with Grandfather Fitzgerald a concern for people in need, and he was generous to those who came into his tavern needing a handout.

Bobby was born in the decade called the Roaring Twenties—a time of relative prosperity in the United States. His dad prospered along with the nation. By the age of twenty-five, Joe Kennedy was the youngest bank president in the United States. By the time of Bobby's birth, he had become a millionaire. He made money in several enterprises, including real estate and the stock market. Three months after Bobby's birth, his father entered the motion picture business. Joe Sr. had "a phenomenal genius head," exclaimed one family friend.[3]

Joe Sr. was at the center of Kennedy family life. He imparted his own extraordinary ambition to each of his children. In matters of child rearing, Joe and Rose were in perfect agreement. They valued competition, enterprise, victory. "I don't want any sourpusses around here," he told the children. "Don't come in second or third—that doesn't count—but win." In his life, there was nothing more valuable to him, no asset greater, than his children.[4]

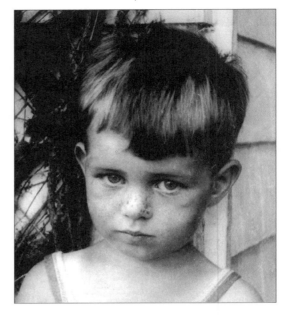

A young Bobby Kennedy
JOHN F. KENNEDY LIBRARY

Away on frequent trips, he always returned home a conquering hero with gifts and stories about his many celebrity friends, among them cowboy movie star Tom Mix, baseball giant Babe Ruth, and football running back Red Grange.

Bobby was only a toddler in 1927 when his father escorted the family on board a private railroad car and traveled to the Riverdale section of the Bronx, New York, where he had bought a home.

Although the Kennedys left Boston in splendor, there was one unpleasant note. Joe Sr. had not achieved his driving goal to enter the inner circle of Boston's high society, its Protestant Yankee world. Members of the Cohasset Country Club had refused him membership because he was an Irish Catholic.

Every time Joe Sr. saw signs in Boston storefront windows that proclaimed NO IRISH NEED APPLY, he felt the sting of prejudice. "I felt it was no place to bring up Irish Catholic children," he said.[5]

He left for another reason too. "If you want to make money, go where the money is," he said. The money was in New York, and Joe Sr. was out to accumulate a fortune. He believed that his acceptance into Yankee aristocracy would come through the accumulation of wealth.[6]

Joe Sr. bought a twenty-room mansion with gracious old elm trees on a six-acre lot with a cottage for the chauffeur and gardener. Shortly after the move, he bought vacation homes in Hyannisport, Massachusetts, and in Palm Beach, Florida.

As her husband's fortunes grew, Rose hired more household staff, including cooks, chauffeurs, gardeners, nurses and governesses. She surrounded her children with private instructors. There were tutors and coaches for schoolwork, sailing, calisthenics, swimming, piano, and dancing.

Rose spent much more time with Rosemary, nearest to Jack in age, than with any of her other children. Rose worked hard to teach her to use a fork, to learn the alphabet, and to steer a sled. Often Rose worried about the toll that working with Rosemary took on her other children. Rosemary had been born retarded. For years, the family kept Rosemary's problem a closely guarded secret.

Just as the children were "rocked to political lullabies," they were also rocked to the ebb and flow of the tides. Bobby's favorite family residence was in Hyannisport. This was the place he considered home, no matter where he was.

The sea was his refuge. The ocean brought the Kennedy children even closer together. They enjoyed the scent of the salt and the sea, the feel of grainy sand beneath their feet, the tall wild grasses hugging the shoreline, the screeching of herring gulls, the fragile diaphanous shells of fledgling horseshoe crabs.

At the age of four, Bobby threw himself into the cold, windswept waters of Nantucket Sound from the family sailboat in a determined effort to learn to swim. Joe Jr. rescued Bobby, who was gulping and shivering. "It showed either a lot of guts or no sense at all, depending on how you look at it," Jack said later.

In Palm Beach, Bobby (at right in swimsuit) poses with his father, his sisters Pat (top) and Jean, and his youngest brother, Teddy. JOHN F. KENNEDY LIBRARY

Luck wasn't always on his side. Once his sister Eunice scooped up a gob of chocolate icing and hurled it at Bobby across the table. Startled and furious, he chased Eunice and darted blindly toward her at full speed. When she stepped adeptly aside, he hit his head hard against the table. The wound required several stitches.

Even more serious was the time a boy hit him in the eye with hot tar. For days, his vision was badly blurred, and Bobby and his family worried that he would lose his sight. Fortunately, there was no permanent damage. "A very narrow escape," his father wrote in a letter to Joe Jr.[7]

In the noisy, bustling, roaring family, young Bobby was clumsy and awkward. Once at a formal party, he snatched a glass of tomato juice from a serving tray, and the juice splattered everywhere—floor, ceiling, and on the formal attire of the guests. Bobby constantly dropped things, bumped into furniture, and was prone to accidents. And his openness and naiveté made him easy to tease and order around.

Bobby was not only sandwiched between five girls (Jean, the eighth child and fifth daughter, was born on February 20, 1928) but he was eclipsed by his gregarious and popular younger brother, Edward Moore, called Teddy, born seven years after Bobby on February 22, 1932. Teddy, the baby of the family, was a scene-stealer, a pudgy, cuddly entertainer.

But Bobby's driving desire was to live up to his three older siblings—Joe Jr., Jack, and Kathleen. They were "the pick of the litter," said one friend. Bright, confident, and handsome, they were "a golden trio."

Joe Jr. declared that one day he would become president, and his family believed him. Jack was proving himself as the Kennedy intellectual, and Kick, "the sunshine" of her family, had "an infectious laugh that projected like a kind of tinkling sound, like the bells on the cows in a mountainside field." She was witty and popular.[8]

His older brothers were his heroes. Joe Jr. and Jack taught Bobby to sail and to play football, but try as he might to imitate their athletic grace and ease, in most matters he fell short. He was not only considerably younger than they were but he was the least coordinated, the least able to put into words what he was thinking. When his older brothers stalked and provoked each other, Bobby clasped his hands over his ears and huddled with his sisters upstairs as the two older boys battled on the living-room floor. Joe Jr., older, bigger, and stronger, always came out on top. Jack inevitably lost.

Bobby understood early what it meant to be an underdog. Also, although he did not like reading or writing, Bobby was drawn to the stories that his brother told him. Jack knew how to spin a good yarn, and Bobby waited excitedly for him to return from school. The two boys would go for a walk, and Jack's stories would hold Bobby spellbound.

Joe Sr. was occasionally impatient and rough with Bobby. Action was his father's byword. He was outraged by idleness. Bobby worked tirelessly to live up to his parents' expectations, but he sensed that his father was more devoted, attentive, and affectionate toward his older brothers. Bobby fought for a place in his heart.

One day, Bobby was playing in the living room when he heard the call for supper. Wanting to be on time, he made a mad dash for the dining room and careened into a glass door, shattering it. Shards of glass splintered all over, and everyone panicked when they saw Bobby on the floor covered with blood. They took him to the hospital, where he had to have stitches, and Bobby made a quick recovery.

If he was accident-prone, he was also enterprising. Despite the family's wealth, Bobby tried to forge his own fortune. He raised and sold rabbits, owned a pig named Porky (which he planned to breed), and he sold subscriptions to magazines and delivered them in his neighborhood.

He wasn't as successful at school. He stumbled as he struggled to read and write. He was much more inclined to feats of physical daring.

In ten years, Bobby attended twelve schools. Being shuffled from school to school took its toll, doing little for his sagging confidence. Besides, it was not easy for him to make friends. He always felt like the outsider.

At the Kennedy dinner table, where politics was served at every meal, his father challenged the children's grasp of national and world affairs. Bobby had a tough time getting a word in edgewise. He believed that nobody cared what he said, and he began to withdraw.

As he grew older, his warm, expressive blue eyes conveyed an inner world of worry and timidity. He became shy and brooding, and he had difficulty putting into words the depth of his feelings. He became full of curious contradictions. He was shy yet open with his affections, he was reticent yet lively, he had little confidence yet he was full of daring and bravado.

Early in his life, he embarked on a spiritual journey. In preparation for becoming an altar boy at St. Joseph's Church in Bronxville, he studied Latin and the lives of the saints. He identified closely with the teachings of the Roman Catholic church and the life of Jesus Christ. He recited Latin to his sister Pat and to his mother. He learned the church service by heart.[9]

In 1938, when Bobby was twelve, a major change swept through his life. His father was appointed ambassador to England by President Franklin Delano Roosevelt. Bobby left the Riverdale Country School in the Bronx and on March 9 boarded an ocean liner with his mother, his sisters Kick, Pat, and Jean, and his brother Teddy. Joe Sr. had already crossed the Atlantic to assume his new post. Joe Jr. and Jack were studying at Harvard, and Rosemary and Eunice would join the family at the end of the semester.

"This is my first trip to Europe and I'm very excited. I didn't even sleep last night," Bobby said in a filmed interview on board the ocean liner. As the ship left the dock, Bobby floated a parachute out of his stateroom porthole.[10]

The Kennedy family won the hearts of the British people. The British press praised Joe Sr.'s informal style, Rose's youthful appearance and energy, and the exuberance of the nine children. Joe Kennedy was the first Irish-American ambassador to England in the history of the United States—and the first Roman Catholic.

Bobby at age twelve JOHN F. KENNEDY LIBRARY

At their new residence at 14 Prince's Gate near Kensington Garden, Rose organized her staff of twenty-three servants and three chauffeurs. Meanwhile, Bobby and Teddy explored the thirty-six-room mansion with its paintings and sculptures, tried out the telephones connecting each room, and operated the antiquated iron-gated lift. They stared at themselves in the giant floor-to-ceiling mirror in the entrance foyer. Bobby told a reporter from the *Daily Express*, "Brought a lot of books from home. Mostly they're about airplanes. I'm going to learn to fly as soon as possible."[11]

Bobby and Teddy attended the Gibb School, a prep school one mile from the embassy. Often, Luella Hennessey, the family nurse, met the boys after school and walked them home. Each time they passed the Brompton Oratory, the splendid church his family attended, Bobby said, "Let's go in and pay a visit to the Lord." When Bobby noticed that the priests were short on wood for the fireplaces in their living quarters, he told his dad. Joe Kennedy was touched by his son's concern and arranged for a year's supply of wood to be sent to the church.[12]

He refused to join a British Boy Scout troop because he would have to pledge allegiance to the King of England. He held fast to principle. But when his dad arranged for him to join an American troop, he attended the British meetings as a visiting member.

World War II intruded on the Kennedy adventure in England. On September 3, 1939, Britain declared war on Germany, and Bobby nervously watched British children with knapsacks on their backs being evacuated from London. The sound of air raid sirens was shrill in his ears. There was fear and panic in the streets, and Bobby learned how to wear a gas mask in case of enemy attack.

With the danger growing, Joe Sr. decided to send his family home, while he remained in England to perform his duties as ambassador. Bobby and the other family members returned to the United States by ship on September 18, 1939. The boat was overcrowded with passengers anxious to return to the United States. People were sleeping in the lounges, the swimming pool, and on the decks.

Back home, Bobby entered the second form (eighth grade) at St. Paul's School, a posh Protestant preparatory school located in Concord, New Hampshire. On October 6, 1939, he transferred to Portsmouth Priory in Portsmouth, Rhode Island, a Catholic boarding school run by Benedictine monks.

Portsmouth Priory had strict requirements: courses in Christian doctrine and church liturgy; religious conferences and retreats; morning chapel and weekly sermons. After three years there, Bobby still had poor grades, and his father decided that another change was in order. "The boy is spending far too much time on religious subjects and not enough on academics," Joe Sr. said. "That's what will get him into Harvard, the religion won't."[13]

Bobby transferred to Milton Academy in Massachusetts in September 1942 as a junior. Bobby was not an outstanding student at Milton. "He was not gifted either academically or socially or athletically," said his classmate David Hackett, "but I think he wanted to excel, and he had a great determination to do well at anything he tried."[14]

"It's no wonder his grades are so low," Albert Norris, Milton housemaster, told Bobby's father. "He no sooner gets in a school situation than he is pulled out, put into a new school situation, with different rules and regulations. He has no roots. He is always on the move."[15]

At times, preoccupied with their own lives, his siblings seemed to forget that Bobby was around. Once, after he had been away at school, he looked forward to returning home and to seeing his family. He entered the house, and Jack was with some friends in the living room. The group was immersed in conversation, and as Bobby approached, they were totally oblivious to him. As he started up the stairs, he called out to his brother, "Aren't you going to even say hello?"

At about this time, he wrote a letter to his father: "I wish Dad that you would write me a letter as you used to Joe and Jack about what you think about the different political events and the war as I'd like to understand what's going on better than I do now." His father answered enthusiastically in an informative letter defining his views on Europe and the Far East.

Bobby was elated. "Thanks very much for your letter, Dad, which is just what I wanted."

At Milton Academy, he was not popular for several reasons: He didn't like raw, off-color jokes, and if he was around when one was being told, he would raise his eyebrows or clam up. He had no inclination toward small talk or idle conversation. Some classmates considered him dull and boring; others thought him rude, cranky, and self-righteous. He was a transfer student and a Catholic. Most students were Protestants and had been at Milton for a long time. They saw Bobby as an outsider. That's how he viewed himself.

Still, he made two loyal friends at Milton, David Hackett and Samuel Adams. Dressed in his usual gray flannel pants, white athletic socks, and flamboyant tie, Bobby walked a mile and a half to attend the nearest Catholic church. Sometimes, he corralled Dave or Sam to join him. They both recognized that he was a devout Catholic emboldened by his belief in God. "His absolute faith in God also gave him faith in himself and appeared to make him oblivious to his lack of popularity among many of his class-mates," Sam Adams said.[16]

The war took a devastating toll on Bobby and his family. Jack sustained a severe back injury after a Japanese destroyer rammed his PT boat in the South Pacific in 1943. But it was Joe Jr., a navy pilot, who would be mourned. On August 12, 1944, Joe Jr. was killed in a secret mission over the English Channel.

Just months before, Bobby had visited his oldest brother at his naval air station in Norfolk, Virginia. Joe Jr. had secretly hustled Bobby into the copilot's seat of his aircraft, coaching him in flying and encouraging him to take the controls. Exhilarated by the challenge, Bobby piloted the plane.

Bobby was crushed by his brother's death. For days, he walked around lost and bewildered. Indeed, the whole Kennedy family reeled. Rose described the days and weeks after Joe Jr.'s death as "the blackest hours of [my] life." Joe Sr. suffered a crisis of faith that would take him years to over-come. "You know how much I had tied my whole life up to his and what great things I saw in the future for him," he wrote to a friend. Joe Sr. never recovered from the death of his firstborn son.

Profoundly touched by his brothers' heroism and haunted by the tragic loss of men in war, Bobby hungered for action. In November 1944, Bobby reported to the navy V-12 unit at Bates College in Lewiston, Maine, for specialized officer training with the U.S. Navy, but he became bored and restless. "My usual moody self. I get very sad at times," he wrote.

He made a special appeal for active duty to Navy Secretary James Forrestal, a friend of his father. On February 1, 1946, Bobby was assigned to duty on the *Joseph P. Kennedy Jr.*, a 2,200-ton destroyer named in honor of his brother. But the war was now over, and Bobby never saw the kind of action

With his father looking over his shoulder, Bobby is sworn in to the U.S. Navy. JOHN F. KENNEDY
LIBRARY

he craved. As a seaman apprentice, he worked on the upkeep of the ship off the coast of Cuba, hosing the desk and chipping paint. On May 30, 1946, Bobby received an honorable discharge from the navy.

Joe Sr. wanted to see his sons excel in the public arena, in politics. Now that his hope for his firstborn son to become president of the United States had been shattered, he turned to his second son, urging Jack to enter the political fray. Jack was hesitant, but he complied. "If Joe were alive, I wouldn't be in this. I'm only trying to fill his shoes," Jack told voters in Massachusetts's eleventh congressional district.

Bobby assisted his brother in his first campaign for Congress. Jack, unsure of himself as a political candidate, also seemed unsure whether Bobby would do his campaign any good. "It's damn nice of Bobby wanting to help," Jack said to a friend, "but I can't see that sober, silent face breathing new vigor into the ranks." One campaign worker recommended that Bobby be assigned East Cambridge, where they expected to lose by a large majority. "The kid can't do any harm there," he said. But Bobby threw himself into the campaign with characteristic vigor. He campaigned in three working-class wards in Cambridge "as if his life depended on it." In November 1946, Jack won his first bid for political office.[17]

After his brother's election, Bobby returned to Harvard, where he had enrolled earlier in the fall. At Harvard, he showed little interest in study and scholarship, and he was placed on probation. All of his energy, determination, and zeal were spent on the football field. In a practice game, Bobby crashed into an equipment wagon while trying to block an opposing player. He staggered to his feet and went back to his position as end and kept playing until he collapsed and was carried from the field. An X-ray revealed that Bobby had broken his leg.

Ultimately, however, Bobby's tenacity earned him a Harvard letter; he was the only Kennedy boy to achieve this distinction. At last, Bobby had done something that earned him a measure of his father's respect.

While at college, a brief stint as a summer employee in his dad's bank, the Columbia Trust Company, had a marked influence on Bobby. His job was to collect rents from poor people in East Boston. The work took him into one of Boston's poverty pockets, and he was startled by what he saw: people who couldn't make enough money for their next meal, who were poor and downtrodden and lived in tenements crawling with rats.

After graduating from Harvard, twenty-two-year-old Bobby traveled to Europe and the Middle East on a trip planned by his father. When Lord Beaverbrook met Bobby in England, he wrote Joe Sr., "He is a remarkable boy. He is clever, has a good character, energy, a clear understanding, and a fine philosophy." Joe Sr. responded, "He is just starting off and has the difficulty of trying to follow two brilliant brothers, Joe and Jack. That in itself is

The only Kennedy boy to earn a varsity letter for football, Bobby (bottom right) is shown here with the Harvard team. ROBERT F. KENNEDY MEMORIAL

Tel-Aviv, Israel, was a high point of Bobby's adventure-filled trip to the Middle East.
ROBERT F. KENNEDY MEMORIAL

quite a handicap and he is making a good battle against it." Slowly but surely, Bobby was winning his father's esteem.[18]

From the Middle East, Bobby filed reports on the Arab-Israeli war for the *Boston Post*. Israel, conforming to a United Nations mandate, had proclaimed its independence. The United States had formally recognized the new nation, but almost immediately Israel was invaded. The site was a tinderbox of hatred and violence.

Bobby planned to travel the dangerous stretch from Tel Aviv to Jerusalem in a convoy of trucks. When an Israeli tank captain invited him to join him, Bobby accepted. The truck convoy was blown to bits by Arab raiders, and all were killed. The tank made it through safely. Luck was on Bobby's side.[19]

When Bobby returned from Europe, he enrolled at the University of Virginia Law School. As head of the student forum, he organized several speeches by prominent Americans, including his father and his brother Jack. A black person had never been allowed to make a speech at the segregated university, but Bobby invited Ralph Bunche, an African American diplomat, to speak. Bobby fought against the protests of the college and made a persuasive case for Ralph Bunche's participation and won.

Bobby's own public performance was less remarkable than his backstage politicking. In his introduction of the speakers, he was shaky and self-conscious. His voice was high-pitched with a nasal twang. His remarks struck his listeners as flat and lifeless.

These years had continued to be difficult for the Kennedy family. In May 1948, the third of the golden trio, his sister Kathleen Kennedy Hartington, along with her lover Peter Fitzwilliam, was killed in a plane crash in Europe. When he heard the news, Bobby broke down and cried.

Yet, during his law school years, Bobby's personal life began to flourish. On a ski slope in Mont Tremblant in Quebec, Canada, Bobby stumbled across a lively young woman named Ethel Skakel. Ethel had been his sister Jean's college roommate at Manhattanville College of the Sacred Heart.

Bobby had occasionally dated Ethel Skakel's older, more serious sister Pat. But, in time, it was Ethel who won his heart. On weekends, Bobby visited the high-spirited young student at Manhanttanville College, where she majored in English. Ethel and Bobby laughed, played, teased. Outgoing, spontaneous, and irrepressible, Ethel affected Bobby in a way that no one ever had before.

The young couple began to date regularly, but Bobby found Ethel hard to pin down. At one point, she seriously considered becoming a nun as an alternative to marriage. Bobby became anxious. "How can I fight God?" he said forlornly to his sister Jean. His persistence won her over.

Although Rose approved of sparkling-eyed Ethel, she had misgivings about the wedding date. She wanted them to wait until Bobby graduated from law school. But, on June 17, 1950, they were married at St. Mary's Roman Catholic Church in Greenwich, Connecticut. Jack Kennedy was Bobby's best man. After a lavish reception at the Skakel family estate and a honeymoon in Hawaii, Ethel and Bobby settled in Charlottesville, where he entered his final year of law school.

Bobby graduated from the University of Virginia Law School in June 1951. On July 4, 1951, Ethel gave birth to their first child, Kathleen Hartington, named after his deceased sister. Their second child was born September 24, 1952, and named Joseph Patrick Kennedy II, after Bobby's brother who had died a hero's death in World War II. Marrying Ethel Skakel changed Bobby's life. He seemed more relaxed and easier on himself. He laughed more and his confidence soared.

Like his brother Jack, he paid little attention to clothes. And like Jack, money was something he didn't need to be bothered about. But unlike Jack, it was not

Bobby Kennedy and Ethel Skakel during their whirlwind courtship ROBERT F. KENNEDY MEMORIAL

The newlyweds celebrate their marriage. JOHN F. KENNEDY LIBRARY

until Bobby completed his formal education that he began to become interested in reading and literature.

He landed a great job as a lawyer at the Justice Department in Washington, D.C. The world looked bright to Bobby. The future seemed in his hands. But he was at the Justice Department only a short time when he received an urgent call that Jack's campaign for U.S. senator from Massachusetts was a ragtag mess and needed him. Bobby reluctantly gave up his first real job to manage his brother's campaign. "I owe it to my brother Jack to return to Massachusetts and do my part before the Democratic primary in September," he said. Bobby hurried home.

chapter two

The Investigator
(1952–1959)

I am become a name.

When it came to running a political campaign, Bobby Kennedy was still a novice. Sure, in 1946 when Jack first entered politics, Bobby pitched in and knocked on doors. In the poorest, most anti-Kennedy district of Cambridge, Bobby's earnestness won affection and votes.

But that was virtually his entire political experience, and now he was in the thick of a campaign in a state where he had lived for very few of his twenty-seven years. Still, Bobby was positive that he knew how to do things better than the veteran workers. As far as he was concerned, there was no magic to politics. The secret was to put in long hours, something he felt the old-timers were unwilling to do.

"If you're not going to work, don't hang around here," he snapped to one longtime Massachusetts politician. He had little respect for these local "pols." They were Irish American like his own family, but he was impatient with their habit of chatting leisurely among themselves and their constituents. He interpreted their behavior as laziness. "Politicians do nothing but hold meetings," he complained. "You can't get any work out of a politician."[1]

No one accused Bobby Kennedy of laziness. He worked eighteen-hour days on the campaign trail, throwing himself into every aspect of the organization. One day, he scrambled up an extension ladder and perched precariously on the top rung to nail a sign reading ELECT JOHN F. KENNEDY TO THE U.S. SENATE.

Hard work, however, was not the only source of Bobby's drive and power. Bobby proved to be a master at organization. He orchestrated a network of committees to write letters, ring doorbells, and register voters. Kennedy for Senator headquarters sprang up in every town in Massachusetts. He was also the member of the Kennedy children who was best at handling their father. Joe Kennedy had helped launch Jack's political career. Six years later, he still wanted to run the show. Bobby was skillful at taking good advice from his father, but he made sure that Jack was able to preserve some needed independence from Joe's dominance.

Some people who worked on the campaign found that they simply didn't like Bobby Kennedy. He struck them as a cocky young kid straight out of law school. His very intensity and brashness, however, were also valuable campaign tools. Bobby conducted fierce negotiations with the governor of Massachusetts, Paul Dever, who was withholding his support for Jack at a crucial moment in the campaign. "Keep that fresh kid of yours out of my sight from here on in," Dever said to Bobby's father.

Bobby's target was not Paul Dever but victory for his war-hero brother in the upcoming election. His motives seemed selfless. "I don't care if anybody around here likes me," he said, "as long as they like Jack."

The campaign was both exhilarating and exhausting. John Fitzgerald Kennedy faced long odds, running against a popular Republican incumbent, Henry Cabot Lodge Jr., who was a member of one of the oldest and most powerful families in the state. Furthermore, the Republicans had Dwight David Eisenhower, an enormously popular World War II general, on their ticket for president, and this would help local Republican candidates as well.

When victory came in November 1952, it was a moment for Bobby Kennedy to savor. The family had won a crucial campaign. Jack was no longer just one of 435 members of the U.S. House of Representatives, but one of ninety-six U.S. senators and a national figure to be reckoned with. The campaign had also brought the brothers together in a new and dynamic way—as fellow adults, engaged in a common mission.

But the victory belonged to Jack. He was an elected United States senator. "What are you going to do now?" Joe Kennedy barked at Bobby as soon as the campaign was over. "Are you going to sit on your tail end and do nothing for the rest of your life? You'd better go out and get a job."[2]

As it turned out, Joe helped steer Bobby toward a job that would cast a shadow over the rest of the decade and the rest of his life. He put his son in touch with one of his friends, a powerful Republican senator from Wisconsin named Joseph McCarthy. In early 1953, McCarthy hired Bobby Kennedy as a staff attorney for the Senate's Permanent Subcommittee on Investigations. Ethel Kennedy packed up their modest belongings and the couple's two children, and the family headed to Washington, D.C.

Investigations. It sounded like a thrilling opportunity for a young attorney. He would probe into dark secrets. He would expose people and organizations who were a threat to national security. He would prove his mettle.

In the 1950s, many Americans believed that the main threat to the United States stemmed from one principal source, a force they called Communism. During the earlier part of the twentieth century, followers of the philosopher Karl Marx had developed a system of government in which there were great restrictions on owning private property, and the central government controlled many aspects of people's lives. Communists believed that their system promoted greater equality, since in theory there would be no rich but also no poor. Those who disliked Communism believed that it was a way of taking away crucial freedoms. The place where Communism had the most repressive force was in the great empire of the Soviet Union, which had grown up around Russia in the eight years since the end of World War II.

Bobby Kennedy's association with Senator Joseph McCarthy later earned him the distrust of many people. LIBRARY OF CONGRESS

In 1953, Senator McCarthy was making his reputation as a man who was protecting the United States from Communists. He believed that the Communist Party had formed a large secret underground organization and that its members were infiltrating the American government. He believed that the aim of the Reds, as the Communists were known, was nothing less than the domination of the United States and the entire world. The Permanent Subcommittee on Investigations was McCarthy's weapon against the Reds. Relying primarily on informants, it sniffed out subversion in places high and low.

Bobby Kennedy's first assignment as assistant counsel to the subcommittee was quite down-to-earth. He was asked to investigate trade between the United States and China, which had also recently undergone a Communist revolution. McCarthy was concerned that Great Britain and other American allies were helping the fledgling Communist regime gain economic power. Bobby Kennedy spent six months producing a creditable, if dull, report.

Bobby was not entirely happy with his position. The major irritation was a man named Roy Cohn, who though even younger than Kennedy was the chief counsel for the subcommittee. Cohn was grasping, power hungry, and vindictive. While Bobby Kennedy was pursuing tedious foreign policy questions, Roy Cohn was targeting individuals inside the United States as Communists.

With Cohn's prodding, the subcommittee was snooping into the past activities of people in government, business—even the movies. If there was a shred of evidence that someone had the slightest contact with the Communist Party, that person was brought before the committee and asked to name those friends who were or ever had been Communists. If there was no evidence, the committee sometimes leaked gossip and innuendoes to the press. Critics of this style of investigation, which came to be called McCarthyism, compared the committee's tactics to a witchhunt.

Kennedy disliked Cohn and his uncouth methods so intensely that, in July 1953, he quit the committee. At his father's urging, he joined the respected Hoover Commission on Reorganization of the Executive Branch as his father's assistant. The commission was charged with studying the federal government and its bureaucracy. But Bobby became impatient and restless with bickering among committee members. His role on the committee seemed minuscule. He needed a job where he could make a difference.

After six months, he was back on the Permanent Subcommittee on Investigations, although the situation had changed. This time, instead of being hired by Joe McCarthy, he was asked by the Democratic senators on the committee to be minority counsel. He hoped that this would give him a measure of freedom from Roy Cohn's excesses.

Nevertheless, it was a precarious situation. Throughout 1954, McCarthy and Cohn continued to haul witnesses before the committee, trampling on their rights and thus degrading the United States Constitution. As minority counsel, Kennedy was able to help keep the Republicans on the committee in check by preparing questions for the Democratic senators.

In June, his conflict with Roy Cohn flared up into open warfare, as the two men clashed over Cohn's rough treatment of a witness. Cohn stormed over to Kennedy, brandishing the witness's file like a weapon. "Do you want to fight right here?" Cohn demanded. Bobby Kennedy simply turned away. The newspapers had a field day: "Cohn, Kennedy Near Blows in 'Hate' Clash," read one headline.[3]

By the end of 1954, however, McCarthy's power was on the decline. The public outcry against his tactics was growing, and even his colleagues in the Senate were becoming fed up. In December, the Senate voted a formal censure of Joseph McCarthy for his abuse of congressional authority in the subcommittee's work. While carrying no actual penalties, a censure was a stern public rebuke.

Midterm elections in the fall of 1954 gave the Democrats a majority in the U.S. Senate. An Arkansas Democrat, John L. McClellan, was named the new chairman of the Permanent Subcommittee on Investigations. Bobby Kennedy was now no longer a bit player and he took over for Roy Cohn as the chief counsel to the committee. He would be able to play a part in returning the committee to its more legitimate investigative work.

Although Kennedy disliked McCarthy's tactics, he could never bring himself to dislike Joe McCarthy. Even as others began to shun the Republican senator, Bobby Kennedy, to some degree, remained loyal. After all, Joe McCarthy was a friend of his father and the godfather of Kathleen, Bobby's first child. He was also the man who essentially had given him his start in government service.

McCarthy's health began to fail soon after his censure. He was drinking heavily, and sometimes he even appeared drunk at committee hearings. When McCarthy died in May 1957, Bobby Kennedy wrote in his journal, "It was all very difficult for me as I feel that I have lost an important part of my life—even though it is in the past." He was one of the few people from Washington who traveled to Appleton, Wisconsin, for Joe McCarthy's funeral.[4]

Many friends and colleagues wondered how Bobby Kennedy could have allowed himself to be associated with a man who destroyed so many lives. Even though Bobby never personally participated in the hectoring and persecution that made the McCarthy committee infamous, he had played a part in one of the darkest moments in American history.

During these years, Ethel Kennedy ate two dinners each night—one at 6:30 P.M. with her children, the other after 10:00 P.M., when her husband returned from Capitol Hill. Robert Kennedy was a tireless worker, and he frequently stayed at the office long into the night. He loved to clown with the clan on weekends, but during the week, being a father took second place to his driving commitment to his work.

The family was growing by leaps and bounds. Ethel had been pregnant with Kathleen while Bobby was slogging through his last year of law school. Joseph Patrick Kennedy II was born during the heat of Jack's 1952 campaign for the Senate. Robert Kennedy Jr. was born in early 1954, shortly after his father was named chief counsel for the Subcommittee on Investigations. Before the decade was over, David, Courtney, and Michael would join the family.

It was a big family, but Bobby himself had come from a family of nine children, and both Bobby and Ethel thrived on the chaotic, topsy-turvy style that they adopted for their household.

Money was not a problem. Bobby's salary was modest, but Joseph Kennedy had given each of his children a million dollars outright. He wanted his children to be free of financial concerns. That way they would be able to pursue public service without worrying about providing for their families.

Because of Bobby's jam-packed schedule, Ethel managed the household and took responsibility for raising their children. Bobby had made a conscious choice to throw himself completely into his work.

Closeness among the larger Kennedy family remained important to Bobby. The senate campaign had deepened his relationship with Jack. Proximity in Washington, D.C., gave the brothers an opportunity to work together. Bobby's youngest brother, Teddy, also visited Washington frequently, and the brothers maintained their tradition of touch football wherever they could find a field.

Sometimes finding a place to play was not so easy. On one of Teddy's visits, the brothers were sharing a field with a group of baseball players from Georgetown University. The college hitters were launching long fly balls right into the Kennedy family game. Ted asked them to stop. The baseball players refused, and a bloody brawl ensued. Bobby jumped in vigorously to protect his brother and his turf. "That must have been a rough game of catch," Ethel commented when Bobby came home that night.[5]

Loyalty was one of Bobby Kennedy's cardinal commitments. When Jack's wife, Jackie, lost her first baby to a miscarriage in 1956, it was Bobby who raced to her hospital bedside. (Jack Kennedy was vacationing with his father in France.) Jackie prized her brother-in-law's comfort and support. Although his work usually prevented him from putting family first, he responded to crisis with vigor.

Jackie Kennedy's misfortune prompted one major change for Bobby Kennedy's family. After losing her baby, Jackie found it too sad to live in the stately, antebellum Virginia home where she and Jack had hoped to start a large family. In 1957, Jack sold the house, called Hickory Hill, to his younger brother.

The move from a cramped townhouse in the urban Washington, D.C., neighborhood of Georgetown to the five-acre country estate liberated the growing family. Now, there was always a field available for touch football and for the rough-and-tumble fun that Bobby enjoyed on weekends. As if a half-dozen children (to start) weren't enough, the family began adopting animals. By 1958, three dogs, a horse, a pony, a burro, a pig, six rabbits, and six chicks were in residence at Hickory Hill. "When we first moved in," Bobby Kennedy told a *Life* magazine reporter, "it looked big enough. Now it isn't, but we can add wings."

Under the new leadership of Senator John McClellan, the Permanent Subcommittee on Investigations moved away from Joe McCarthy's obsessive pursuit of Communists. Bobby Kennedy became the driving force behind a new arena of investigation. He began chasing down reports that organized crime, "the Mob," was involved in the most powerful American labor union, the Teamsters. Between 1956 and 1959, rooting out this evil became an obsession for Robert Kennedy.

Unions had gotten their start in the United States in the late nineteenth century. During that period, national corporations had developed and grown larger and more powerful. In industries like steel manufacturing and later the automobile industry, labor unions helped protect plumbers, steamfitters, clerks, and factory and warehouse employees from exploitation. Unions played a crucial part in helping gain better pay, more humane working conditions, and job security for the workers on the front lines.

By the 1950s, unions were a powerful force in American life and politics. Millions of workers belonged to unions in many industries. In some cases, however, these organizations that had been started to protect workers from exploitation had begun to take advantage of their own memberships.

This was the case with the Teamsters, which represented workers in the transportation industry, mainly truck drivers. The Teamsters union was so large, well financed, and well organized that it had become a kind of big business of its own. Leadership of the Teamsters union meant more than working to secure the best possible pay for those who drove long-distance rigs. Being a high-ranking Teamster official was a chance to get rich. The leaders no longer always had the best interests of the members at heart.

As the investigations committee's work expanded beyond the pursuit of Communists, Bobby Kennedy began to uncover abuses of power that outraged him. He heard stories of union leaders becoming rich and betraying the interests of their membership. He heard about mobsters infiltrating the Teamsters Union, threatening and sometimes even killing those who opposed their policies. The exploitation of the workers lit a fire within him.

Joseph Kennedy wanted his son to find another cause. Didn't Bobby understand how dangerous challenging the union leadership had become? In addition, the labor unions were strong supporters of the Democratic Party. It was well known that Democrats were friendlier to labor, while Republicans tended to support the interests of business. Even if Bobby's cause was just, Joe reasoned, the investigation of wrongdoing in the unions would harm the Kennedy family's political fortunes. Bobby had not yet shown any interest in running for office himself, but Jack already had his eye on a possible run for president of the United States.

Bobby held his ground. Indeed, he helped convince John McClellan to form a new committee devoted exclusively to the pursuit of corruption in labor. In January 1957, he became chief counsel to the newly formed Senate Select Committee on Improper Activities in the Labor or Management Field. McClellan was chair. One of the members was the junior Democratic senator from Massachusetts, John Fitzgerald Kennedy.

Headquarters were set up in room 101 of the old Senate office building, a suite that soon become littered with the familiar Kennedy clutter. Papers were everywhere, and the telephone began ringing without letup. Bobby Kennedy was in command mode, his collar open, his sleeves rolled up, sometimes even barefoot for maximum comfort. Once the committee was formed and its function made public, members began to receive letters and tips from all over the country. It was clear that many union members were living in fear. Over one thousand letters a week poured into the committee's offices. Many were anonymous. "Please do not use my name—please—I'll be a gone goose if you do," wrote one correspondent. Bobby Kennedy had to distinguish between the genuine, the exaggerated, and the downright fraudulent. "You know there's something very curious I've learned," he told one reporter. "If you get a letter typed on stationery, seven paragraphs in length, and signed by somebody, you can be absolutely sure it's a lie. But if you get a letter which says, 'I saw Jimmy Hoffa take three hundred dollars from somebody in a bar in 1947,' signed 'A Workingman,' it's always true."[6]

The Rackets Committee, as it came to be known, first targeted Dave Beck, president of America's most powerful labor union. Bobby Kennedy and his associates flew out to Seattle and registered in a hotel under assumed names to scope out the situation. Beck, they discovered, had been steadily siphoning off union funds for his own personal use. He had managed to build an expensive home and was living lavishly.

By interviewing a number of people and sifting through mountains

Teamsters official Dave Beck testifies before the McClellan Committee.
LIBRARY OF CONGRESS

of union documents, Bobby Kennedy built a case against Dave Beck. In March 1957, the Rackets Committee called Beck to testify. With Beck on the stand, Bobby Kennedy had his first real chance to assume a starring role as a cross-examiner.

Kennedy felt almost sorry for the union leader. Beck's eyes, once darting pinpoints of light, were downcast. Bobby knew that the evidence against Beck was enough to destroy him, and for a moment he could taste the defendant's defeat and humiliation. But his fierce legal instincts took over, and he began a relentless series of questions that brought to light the full extent of Beck's mishandling of funds. The union leader was forced to take the fifth amendment: "I refuse to answer that question on the grounds that it may incriminate me." Beck eventually went to prison for his misdeeds.

The Beck investigation was only a warm-up. The Rackets Committee's real target was a rising leader named James Riddle Hoffa, who was poised to take over as president of the entire International Brotherhood of Teamsters. Unlike some of the union leadership, Hoffa had begun his career as a truck driver. He was scrappy and smart, a short, compactly built man who carefully cultivated his image as a tough guy.

To prop up that image, he had surrounded himself with a colorful collection of hoodlums. There were men like "Tony Ducks" Corallo (so-called because his friends said that he ducked convictions after his arrests); John Ignazio Dioguardi, called Johnny Dio; and Barney Baker, a 325-pound former boxer. Another of Hoffa's associates was Frank Kierdorf, who served a term for armed robbery in Michigan. When Kierdorf was released, Hoffa put him in charge of a local union in Flint, Michigan, where he initiated a reign of terror against small businessmen who refused to cater to Teamster demands. Kierdorf's crimes ended when he accidentally burned himself to death while setting a fire in a Flint cleaning establishment. These men, with their well-known ties to the Mafia, made Hoffa not only powerful but feared. To cross Jimmy Hoffa was to put your life on the line.

Dave Beck, when challenged, had simply collapsed. Jimmy Hoffa was a fighter. He would match Bobby Kennedy's combativeness every step of the way.

Kennedy and Hoffa first met on a snowy night in February 1957, not in a hearing room but at a dinner party in a private home. The meeting was arranged by Eddie Cheyfitz, a prominent Washington attorney who represented Hoffa but also had ties to the Kennedy family. By bringing the men together, Cheyfitz hoped to convince Bobby Kennedy that Hoffa wasn't so terrible and that prosecuting him would be a waste of time.

Before leaving for Cheyfitz's house, Bobby joked with Ethel about Jimmy Hoffa and his mobster friends. He was a rough, menacing bully, he told her. Ethel laughed, but underneath the laughter, she seemed worried.

At Cheyfitz's house, the two men were polite to each other, but Hoffa boasted repeatedly that he was tough, that he had destroyed employees who had crossed him, that he had broken anybody who stood in his way. He claimed that as a union leader he was simply looking out for his men and keeping a watch on his enemies. "I do to others what they do to me, only worse," Hoffa told Kennedy.

"Maybe I should have worn my bulletproof vest," Bobby responded.

At Hickory Hill, as the evening progressed, Ethel became increasingly anxious. At 9:30 P.M. she called Cheyfitz's house to find out whether every-

James Hoffa was Bobby Kennedy's personal nemesis during the Rackets Committee hearings.
LIBRARY OF CONGRESS

thing was okay. "I'm still alive, dear," Bobby told her. "But if you hear a big explosion, I probably won't be."

When the dinner party ended, Jimmy Hoffa urged Bobby, "Tell your wife I'm not as bad as everyone thinks I am." Bobby Kennedy, however, concluded that Hoffa was even worse than he had imagined. He believed that a man who constantly had to prove himself was dangerous.[7]

Hoffa, for his part, suspected that the young, rich lawyer was looking down on him. "I can tell by how he shakes hands what kind of fellow I got," he told one writer. "Here's a fella thinks he's doing me a favor by talking to me."[8]

That very same month, Kennedy and Hoffa were engaged in a deadly game. When the Rackets Committee was formed, Hoffa hired a man named John Cye Cheasty to act as a spy on the committee's work. He wanted to stay a step ahead by seeing the documents the committee was working with before they came to light. But, in a stroke of good fortune for Kennedy, Cheasty appeared in his office and told the chief counsel what the union leader was planning. Kennedy hired Cheasty as a double agent, and they began to feed Hoffa harmless information that would not jeopardize the committee's work.

Hoffa's attempts to spy on the committee were patently illegal, and Kennedy thought he had a chance to catch him red-handed. So, with Cheasty's help, Kennedy set a trap. In March 1957, the police caught Hoffa on a street in Washington, D.C., stuffing two thousand dollars in Cheasty's pockets and accepting a folder full of "secret" documents.

Bobby was elated, thinking he had scored a major victory over a man who in his mind was a prototype of evil. He rushed down to the police station. There, Hoffa, still determined to prove his superiority, challenged Kennedy to a push-up contest. When Hoffa lost, he claimed that it was because the young attorney was so skinny: "What the hell does it take to lift a feather?" he scoffed.[9]

The next day, Kennedy trumpeted the nabbing of Hoffa to the national press. He was completely convinced that he had Hoffa nailed, and he was not about to miss his chance in the limelight.

"What will you do if Hoffa is acquitted?" one reporter asked.

"I'll jump off the roof of the Capitol," Kennedy replied.[10]

Kennedy, however, spoke too soon. Hoffa was charged with bribery and conspiracy. Kennedy, as an employee of the Senate, had no direct responsibility for prosecuting Hoffa in district court. Nevertheless, he knew that the outcome would be a reflection on his own work, since he had engineered the trap. He found that he had underestimated Hoffa's wiliness. With the help of one of the best criminal lawyers in town, Edward Bennett Williams, Hoffa set out to convince the jury of his sterling character. Eight members of the jury were black, and Williams brought in the famous African American boxer Joe Louis to tell the court how much the union leader had done for his country.

On July 19, 1957, the jury brought in its verdict: not guilty. Jimmy Hoffa's lawyer offered to send Bobby Kennedy a parachute. Four months later, Jimmy Hoffa was formally elected president of the International Brotherhood of Teamsters.

Armed with the Rackets Committee's subpoena power, Bobby was able to continue to grill Hoffa in public over the next two years. Side by side with his brother Jack, he brought Teamster crimes to light, even without securing a conviction. Bobby developed a skill and a reputation as a dogged and informed questioner. His staff did extensive background research, so he seldom asked a question to which he did not already know the answer.

With Hoffa on the stand, Kennedy was biting, sometimes even sarcastic, as he exposed the union leader's misdeeds. For his part, Hoffa took refuge in doublespeak. "To the best of my recollection I must recall on my memory I cannot remember," was a typical Hoffa reply. But Kennedy's background work had uncovered a spectrum of misdeeds: phony land deals in Florida that swindled Teamster Union members out of their hard-earned dollars, a pattern of intimidation aimed at those who opposed Hoffa and his tactics, and blatant embezzlement of Teamster funds.

The competition between the two men that had begun with the push-up contest spilled into the hearing room and beyond. One night, leaving his office at 1:00 A.M., Bobby Kennedy drove past Teamster headquarters, where he noticed that Hoffa's office window was lit. If Jimmy Hoffa was still working, then he decided that he ought to be at the office as well. He turned around and headed back for more hours of sifting through Teamster documents.

Eventually, the investigation led to Hoffa's expulsion from the AFL-CIO and to a prison term for conspiring to fix a jury and for diverting union pension funds.

The Rackets hearings helped catapult both Jack and Bobby to national fame. One newsmagazine story profiled "The Amazing Kennedy Brothers," citing their close relationship, their long working hours, and their success in bringing Teamster crimes to light. Jack Kennedy cosponsored a strong bill that required unions to hold elections with secret ballots and to publish comprehensive financial reports. The bill passed the Senate but failed in the House. The hearings were important, however, in helping spur passage by both houses of a solid if slightly weaker bill in 1959.

Despite the notoriety that the hearings had won for him, Bobby Kennedy became discouraged. The limits of the Rackets Committee's power had become clear. In the fall of 1959, he resigned as chief counsel, wrapping up 300 days of public hearings, 20,432 pages of printed testimony for the record, 1,500 witnesses and 2.5 million miles traveled. In the last months of that year, he wrote a book about his work on the Rackets Committee, *The Enemy Within*, which became a best-seller when it was published.

Discouragement was not the only reason Bobby Kennedy left the Rackets Committee. There was another job waiting for him. Years of careful family preparation were coming to a head. Jack Kennedy was getting ready to run for the highest office in the land, and he needed his younger brother.

chapter three

Father and Brother
(1960–1963)

. . . always roaming with a hungry heart . . .

In the presidential campaign, Bobby proved himself a hard-driving quarter-back. He presided over a complex national network, unafraid to challenge the authority of longtime Democratic Party leaders. At the Democratic National Convention in July 1960, he marshaled the campaign team and mounted a state-by-state count of delegates. Jack Kennedy won the Democratic Party nomination on the first ballot—by just fifteen votes. Bobby Kennedy's superb organization was a key factor in pulling it off.

Once Jack Kennedy had won the Democratic nomination, he was pitted in the general election against the Republican candidate, Vice President Richard M. Nixon. If anything, Bobby Kennedy picked up the pace. Once, running into some campaign workers in the Washington, D.C., headquarters, Bobby burst out impetuously, "What are you doing? What are we all doing? Let's get on the road tomorrow. Let's get on the road tomorrow. I want us all on the road tomorrow."[1] Bobby was possessed by the idea of

On the campaign trail for Jack in Wisconsin JOHN F. KENNEDY LIBRARY

victory, and he drove everyone very hard. His reputation for being brash, arrogant, even "ruthless" grew steadily during the campaign. As historian Arthur Schlesinger put it, "John Kennedy recognized that a campaign required a son of a bitch—and that it could not be the candidate. Robert was prepared to do what the candidate should not have done."[2]

Yet, he could also act impulsively when he felt that an important principle was at stake. In October 1960, in the thick of the general campaign, civil rights leader Martin Luther King Jr. was arrested on a trumped-up charge by officials in Georgia. King was taken in handcuffs and leg chains to a state prison, and it was possible that he would be held there indefinitely. Bobby was furious, and he was also worried that King might be lynched by angry whites. Jack Kennedy had called King's wife, Coretta, to offer his support, but Bobby went further. He placed a direct call to the judge and demanded King's release. "I wanted to make clear that I opposed this. I felt it was disgraceful," Bobby said later. Making the call could have alienated white voters in the South—it could even have cost Jack Kennedy the election. But Bobby never regretted his decision to get involved.

On Election Day 1960, Bobby Kennedy manned the phones from the communications center in the family home in Hyannisport. Reports and rumors dribbled in from all over the country. The race was neck and neck, with the margins in many states being just a few thousand or even a few hundred votes. It was not until well into the morning hours, when the results came in from the states on the West Coast, that anyone could say with certainty what the outcome was. John F. Kennedy had been elected president of the United States.

Robert Kennedy had engineered a brilliant victory, but again he was plagued by the question of what to do next. His brother had a job, and he was out of work. He pondered his options. Would it be better to stay alongside Jack and work in his administration in Washington? Or was it time for him to develop his career independently—go back to New York or Massachusetts and carve out his own niche in politics.

John Kennedy didn't let his younger brother stew very long. When Adlai Stevenson and Abraham Ribicoff refused the job of attorney general, JFK offered it to Bobby. But Bobby feared that cries of nepotism—appointing one's own relatives to high office—would stir controversy.

Bobby had been called "a brash young brat who thinks he can ride his brother's coattails." He might admit to brashness, but riding his brother's coattails was not something that he aimed to do. He wanted to identify himself outside the boundaries of family.

But Joe Sr. urged him to consider the cabinet post. He reminded his sons that Jack needed someone he could trust 100 percent. He believed that nobody was better qualified than Bobby.[3]

"Nepotism, my foot!" he barked. "Why would anyone think that Bobby needs a job?" Joe Sr. believed that Jack had everything to gain by appointing Bobby to the cabinet post.[4]

Bobby believed his brother had a lot to lose. "It would be the 'Kennedy Brothers' by the time a year was up, and the president would be blamed for everything we had to do in civil rights; and it was an unnecessary burden to undertake," he said later.[5]

Bobby wavered. He was considering a bid for governor of the state of Massachusetts. He knew his father and brother would be upset, but he had made up his mind. He called Jack and told him he had decided not to accept the position. Jack brushed off Bobby's words. "Well, don't tell me now. I want to have breakfast with you in the morning."[6]

Over bacon and eggs in Jack's Georgetown home, Jack told Bobby, "I need to know that when problems arise I'm going to have somebody who's going to tell me the unvarnished truth, no matter what." Jack discussed some of the other possible candidates for attorney general, but dismissed them all. "Most of these people I have had some cursory contact with. None of them have I had a long-standing close relationship with. I need you in this government."[7]

Bobby finally relented. Before the Senate Judiciary Committee, he answered cries of nepotism and inexperience with grace. In the end, his appointment was confirmed unanimously by the Judiciary Committee, and with just one Republican dissenter in the full Senate. At thirty-five years old, he became the third youngest attorney general in the nation's history.

Once he agreed to take the job, he was determined to prove to the nation that his brother had made the best possible choice. His department had 30,000 employees and a budget of $300 million a year.

He understood his charge clearly: to enforce the law of the land, to advise the chief executive, and to defend the legality of executive actions. He held up honesty and integrity as virtues. He was determined to rid the nation of injustice.

Bobby rallied around him a vigorous and idealistic group of young professionals, among them Byron White, Yale Law School graduate, as deputy

Bobby and Ethel in a motorcade during his term as attorney general JOHN F. KENNEDY LIBRARY

attorney general, and Professor Archibald Cox of the Harvard Law School as solicitor general. He appointed Nicholas Katzenbach to head the Office of Legal Counsel and Burke Marshall as chief of the Civil Rights Division. He appointed John Siegenthaler as his administrative assistant and Edwin Guthman as his press man.

From those on his team, Bobby demanded energy and excellence. In turn, he garnered respect, admiration, and devotion. In meetings, Bobby had the uncanny ability to get to the crux of a messy problem. He said what he meant openly. He trusted his inner circle and could delegate responsibilities. He was not a blamer or a nitpicker, and he stood by each of his inner circle of staff members as a brother.

Early in his administration as he toured the Justice Department, he said to a colleague, "Did it ever occur to you that we don't have many Negroes working here?" Only 10 of 950 Justice Department lawyers were black. He waged a vigorous campaign to recruit more African Americans to work at Justice.

Under Kennedy's leadership, the Justice Department began a swift transformation from a quiet bureaucracy to a lively, activist institution. Bobby Kennedy set a tone of informality and vitality. His tie was often loosened. His tawny hair was usually tousled, and he had the habit of pushing it back with his hand. He leaned forward slightly when he walked, his shoulders hunched, thus looking smaller than his 5 feet 10 inches and 150 pounds.

Bobby held a late-January barbecue in his spacious wood-paneled office for 125 children. He used the large fireplace to cook. When one of his assis-

As attorney general, Bobby brought a spirit of vigor and informality to the Justice Department. Here he celebrates his birthday in his office. JOHN F. KENNEDY LIBRARY

tant attorney generals suggested that the picnic might be an infraction of a building rule, Bobby snorted, "You're getting old and crotchety."[8]

He broke another rule when he began taking his dog, Brumus, to work every day. Brumus was a beautiful, sad-looking Newfoundland. Bobby's love of dogs was well known. Once, he had jumped into wild seas to save the president's dog, and another time, he brought the presidential motorcade to a halt in Washington when a child's mongrel was hit by one of the motorcade cars.

Bobby's informality irritated J. Edgar Hoover, chief of the Federal Bureau of Investigation, who said, "It is ridiculous to have the attorney general walking around the building in his shirtsleeves. Suppose I had a visitor waiting in my anteroom. How could I have introduced him?"[9]

Hoover also demanded Bobby's undivided attention, and at times, Bobby seemed distracted. On one occasion, during a meeting with Hoover, Bobby tossed darts at a dartboard. One of the darts missed and lodged itself into the wood paneling. Hoover held his temper, but later exclaimed, "It was pure desecration . . . the most deplorably undignified conduct."

Bitter political enemies J. Edgar Hoover and Bobby Kennedy pose together in front of the White House.
JOHN F. KENNEDY LIBRARY

Hoover was also appalled by Brumus. A dog in the Justice Department? Hoover complained, and Bobby faced a thirty-day jail sentence and a fifty-dollar fine for violating a regulation that stated "Dogs and other animals, except for Seeing Eye dogs, shall not be brought upon property for other than official purposes." Bobby left Brumus home.[10]

Even in more serious matters, the two men could find no common ground. Hoover had held the directorship of the FBI since 1924, directing during the presidencies of Calvin Coolidge, Herbert Hoover, Franklin Roosevelt, Harry Truman, and Dwight Eisenhower. The imperious director had begun to think of himself as possessing power beyond presidents.

To celebrate Hoover's thirty-eighth year as director of the FBI, the attorney general planned a celebration in his office. Hoover balked. He didn't want a party hosted by Bobby Kennedy and refused to come. The party was held without him, and Bobby's children ate the cake.

Bobby and Ethel's home, Hickory Hill, became almost as famous as the White House. The house was a white brick colonial mansion with a bright red door situated on a gentle hill. The U-shaped driveway was usually crowded with cars. On the grounds were two swimming pools, one with a poolside jukebox. There was a barn for horses and a private movie theater by one of the pools. Swings hung from old hickory trees, and a tree house nestled comfortably in one tree's branches.

Bobby and Ethel were relaxed hosts. Ethel spearheaded foot races, tennis matches, swimming meets. The atmosphere was casual, genial, and competitive. Ethel's energy was as astounding as Bobby's.

One visitor said that walking into the Kennedy house was like walking into a centipede. The children came together, all arms and legs, in a rush toward the visitor in the center of the floor.

The Hickory Hill animal collection was also growing. The menagerie now included a coati, a raccoonlike animal with a long ringed tail, and a pet seal that devoured ten pounds of fish a day.

Once, when Ethel was showing the menagerie to visitors, the coati leaped at her, bit her on the leg, and refused to let go. She screamed and one of the

Hickory Hill, the Virginia estate where Bobby, Ethel, and their family moved in 1957

JOHN F. KENNEDY LIBRARY

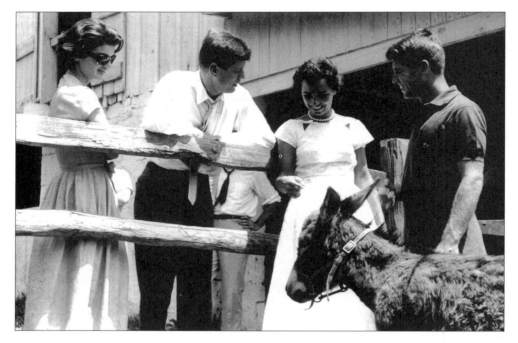

Bobby, Ethel, Jack, and Jackie share a laugh with a donkey, a representative of the Hickory Hill menagerie. JOHN F. KENNEDY LIBRARY

at her, bit her on the leg, and refused to let go. She screamed and one of the visitors wrangled with the animal to loosen its grip.

Bobby welcomed physical challenges, accepting them as tests of his own tenacity and courage. When the president commented that United States marines should be able to hike fifty miles in three days, Bobby acted as if his brother were talking to him. "I think I'll take a fifty-mile hike tomorrow! You're going with me, aren't you?" he asked four friends. Ed Guthman, Dave Hackett, Lou Oberdorfer, and Jimmy Symington joined Bobby on a wintry morning at 5:00 A.M. on a towpath of the Chesapeake and Ohio canal. One by one they dropped out, but Bobby kept walking and accomplished the feat. "You're lucky your brother isn't the president of the United States!" he said to Ed Guthman.[11]

In sports, Bobby was attracted to the element of danger. He skied just on the edge of control at breakneck speed. He reveled in the rough-and-tumble of football. He believed that football trained young boys for the rigors of life.

Bobby constantly challenged his children and guests to foot races, football games, roughhousing of all sorts. Once, Bobby initiated a push-up contest. He licked Kenny O'Donnell, his Harvard College roommate and special assistant to JFK, but was licked in turn by Theodore White, journalist and author. Then, Bobby and Ethel arranged for an arm-wrestling contest between Theodore White and Georgei N. Bolshakov, press officer for the Russian embassy.

When White appeared to be pinning Bolshakov down, Ethel screamed,

Bobby with some of his children and two dogs at Hickory Hill MAGNUM

"We're winning! Our side is winning. We're winning!" When Bolshakov lifted his elbow off the table, she yelled, "You're cheating! You're cheating! He's cheating! He's cheating!" White said that life at Hickory Hill was great fun and quite often "a panorama of life in Washington."

One of Ethel's favorite games was Sardines, a variation of hide-and-seek. When the seeker discovers the person hiding, the seeker joins the hider. One evening, Ethel tucked herself into a clothes closet. When Robert McNamara discovered Ethel and Byron White, he entered the closet, too. By the time Bobby found them, at least fifteen dinner guests came tumbling out of the closet.

At a party for astronaut John Glenn, Ethel built a flimsy, makeshift bridge across the swimming pool with a table set in the middle for herself and Glenn. It invited prankish danger, but John Glenn stayed clear. He scribbled on a paper napkin, "Help! I'm a prisoner at the Kennedys'!" He tied the note to a balloon and set it aloft. But it was the unsuspecting presidential adviser Arthur Schlesinger who ended up in the pool, catapulted in by one of the guests. At times, Bobby would push Ethel in, and Ethel would return the hijinks.

People gathered at the Kennedy house for more than hijinks. Bobby initiated a series of lively evenings, in which a speaker gave a talk and guests fired questions and discussed ideas. The events came to be known as the Hickory Hill seminars. Among the speakers were Al Capp, the creator of the comic strip "Li'l Abner"; Mortimer Adler, the philosopher and educator; Dr. Lawrence S. Kubie, psychiatrist; and John Kenneth Galbraith, economist.

Bobby's appetite for reading increased. In a three-month period between Christmas 1962 and Easter 1963, he read at least ten books, including Barbara Ward's *The Rich Nations and the Poor Nations*, S. F. Bemis's *John Quincy Adams and the Foundations of American Foreign Policy*, and Barbara Tuchman's *The Guns of August*. Some years earlier, Bobby, Jack, and their friend Lemuel Billings had taken a speed-reading course.[12]

A pile of books sat on Bobby's night table. Even as he shaved, he listened

Kerry Kennedy perches on her father's shoulder. JOHN F. KENNEDY LIBRARY

to plays by Shakespeare. His curiosity about history, literature, and philosophy was growing. Bobby seemed to be making up for lost time.

Spirited as the frolics at Hickory Hill were, they did not distract Bobby from the serious matters of state that he and Jack faced in the first months of the new administration. During his campaign, Jack had made some heady promises to the American people, urging the nation to move toward a "new frontier" of social reform and economic growth.

Yet, the New Frontier was barely launched when, in April 1961, President Kennedy agreed to support an invasion of the island nation of Cuba. President Kennedy was worried that the Communist government of Cuba, led by Fidel Castro, posed a threat to the United States. He approved a plan (originally developed under Dwight Eisenhower) to help train Cuban exiles to invade their country and overthrow Castro. But the invasion failed miserably. At the Bay of Pigs (Bahia de los Cochinos), on the coast of Cuba, more than one thousand men were captured and imprisoned.

Bobby Kennedy had not been consulted on the decision to support the Bay of Pigs plan. In fact, he was not even told about the plan until just days before the invasion. Instead, John Kennedy relied on the advice of "experts" whom he barely knew.

After the fiasco, Jack called upon Bobby to help figure out what had gone wrong. He promised his brother that he would always be included in the important decisions of his presidency. From that time on, Bobby Kennedy's role as attorney general expanded well beyond addressing strictly legal issues. Bobby became Jack's most trusted adviser, even when the issues involved military matters and foreign policy.

The Bay of Pigs fiasco led to a more significant crisis with Cuba in October 1962. This time Bobby played a decisive role. The United States and the Soviet Union were brought to the brink of war over the presence in Cuba of Soviet missiles.

Some advisers advocated a surprise military attack—a surgical air strike. "I could not accept the idea," said Bobby, "that the United States would rain bombs on Cuba killing thousands and thousands of civilians in a surprise attack."

Instead of a military attack against such a small nation, Bobby advocated a naval blockade, a quarantine stopping shipments of missiles, warheads, and launching equipment. He was concerned about the loss of life. With the world on the brink of nuclear disaster, Bobby's voice was calm, clear, and lucid. He held out firmly against an air strike directed at the Soviet bases in Cuba.

For a time during the thirteen frightening days of the Cuban Missile Crisis, it appeared that nuclear war was inevitable. But in the end, Soviet premier Nikita Khrushchev backed down, turning his ships around. Bobby Kennedy's coolheaded insistence on military restraint helped save the United States and the world from a potential holocaust.

Always close, Bobby and Jack Kennedy confer about strategy. JOHN F. KENNEDY
LIBRARY

Bobby and Jack were growing closer and closer. Bobby was Jack's confidant, his right-hand man, his second self. They were in many ways remarkably different from each other. Jack was detached, Bobby emotional. Jack appeared relaxed, Bobby tense. But their trust in each other was unequivocal.

In this crisis, Bobby's leadership proved decisive in averting nuclear disaster. In one of the most perilous moments in the nation's history, Bobby emerged as a defining influence. To his good friend Dave Powers, who served as an informal adviser, the president said, "Thank God for Bobby." His decision to make Bobby attorney general was proving to be the smartest appointment he had made.

chapter four

"We Will Move"
Robert Kennedy and Civil Rights
(1960–1963)

I am a part of all that I have met . . .

On a crisp day in March 1961, the attorney general of the United States was in New York City for meetings and the taping of a television interview at CBS studios in midtown Manhattan. That was a common activity for a prominent government official.

After the meeting, however, the attorney general did not step into a limousine to be whisked to La Guardia Airport for the flight back to Washington. Instead, Robert Kennedy walked three and one-half miles north—into the heart of Harlem, one of the largest African American communities in the country. Harlem had a glorious history as a center of African American art, music, and writing, but it was now in the grip of terrible poverty. It could be counted as one of the toughest neighborhoods in the entire United States.

In Harlem, Kennedy stopped to talk—not with government officials but with young people. He met with representatives of three of the area's teenage gangs. These young men spoke to him of their sense that the city and country offered them little hope for a secure future. Jobs were scarce for black people, and outside their neighborhood, they still felt the sting of open racism. Without a fair shot in American society, they were losing the incentive to try to succeed.[1]

As attorney general of the United States, Robert Kennedy had been suddenly thrust into the middle of the most explosive issue in American society in the early 1960s: civil rights. African Americans had been freed from slavery a century before, during the Civil War, but in 1961, an ugly tangle of laws and practices still made blacks second-class citizens of the United States. In many parts of the country, especially in the South, blacks could not sit together with whites in a restaurant. They were forced to use separate waiting rooms in bus stations, separate public restrooms, even separate water fountains. Part of the reason these laws could stay on the books was that a number of states had concocted complicated laws that prevented many African Americans from being able to vote.

During the 1950s, while Robert Kennedy had been rooting out corruption in the labor unions, black leaders had joined with some concerned whites to challenge discrimination in American society. Thanks to their efforts, the Supreme Court had outlawed "separate but equal" schools. African Americans had also won some important local victories, like the Montgomery bus boycott, in which by refusing to ride the buses for a year, they forced the companies to end the policy of making black people sit in the back.

Now, with John Kennedy's election as president, civil rights leaders began to look to Washington for action. Specifically, they looked to the Justice Department. As the chief law enforcement officer in the nation, Robert Kennedy had the responsibility to enforce the laws that protected freedom. It was also his responsibility to lead the fight to strike down laws—like those that discriminated against blacks or any other group—that violated the basic principles of freedom and justice as expressed in the U.S. Constitution.

Walking three and one-half miles north to Harlem was not by itself going to change anything. But Bobby knew that he had to begin to understand the problems that black people faced. Although his family had encountered some discrimination as Irish Americans, his father's fortune had insulated Bobby Kennedy from injustice. "I won't say I stayed awake nights worrying about civil rights before I became attorney general," he said later.[2] Now he had to listen, not so easy a task as it first appeared. A tidal wave of anger and frustration had been building for three centuries among African Americans, as they suffered the brutality of slavery, lynchings, and the more subtle but no less cruel sting of legal and extralegal discrimination. Now that tidal wave was about to engulf the country.

On the issue of civil rights, Bobby Kennedy was a combination of passion and prudence. That combination made just about everyone mad at him. His heartfelt, sweeping insistence on the justice of the cause of protesting blacks infuriated many whites, particularly in the South. But he was also sensitive to political considerations, which slowed down his actions. Many blacks felt that they had been told for too long to "wait" for progress, and the prudent side of the attorney general angered them.

In his first months on the job, Kennedy made some small gestures, like his walk to Harlem. But he was only beginning to learn about civil rights. His first public statement on the issue came in May 1961, in an address to the graduating class at the law school of the University of Georgia.

Choosing Georgia as the locale for his first address on civil rights was no small matter. In the heart of the Deep South, Georgia was an intransigent bastion of discrimination against blacks, and Kennedy fully expected a hostile audience. Indeed, he relished the challenge. Sure enough, protests and anger preceded his arrival. "KENNEDY GO HOME" was scrawled on the sidewalk, and a crowd demonstrated against his appearance.

Inside the hall, among the 1,800 faces in the audience, only one was black. She was Charlayne Hunter, the first African American student ever admitted to the University of Georgia—and she had been accepted only because a federal court had forced the university to admit her.

Kennedy had worked for five weeks on the speech. He knew that his words would be scrutinized not only in Georgia but all over the country, as Americans tried to figure out what stance the new administration would take on civil rights.

What he unfolded before the American people in his talk was a clear statement that rested, above all, on the idea that the United States was a nation of laws. In a sense, he told the Georgia graduates, it didn't matter what they or he believed about a particular issue. Our legal system, he explained, is built on common consent to our system of justice—and discrimination against blacks, or any other group, clearly violated the letter and the spirit of the law of the land.

"I happen to believe that the 1954 decision was right," he told them, speaking about the Supreme Court ruling that demanded racial integration in the country's schools. "But, my belief does not matter—it is the law. Some of you may believe the decision was wrong. That does not matter. It is the law. And we both respect the law. By facing this problem honorably, you have shown to all the world that we Americans are moving forward together—solving this problem—under the rule of law."[3]

The speech was a clear statement of principle—but it also carefully avoided challenging the Southerners directly. What Kennedy did *not* say was as important as his spoken words. He took care not to label the Southern establishment as racist. He did not call for immediate, revolutionary change. He laid out not a program but a method. He encouraged those who wished to end discrimination to pursue their fight for justice through the calm, orderly process of the courtroom.

When Kennedy's speech came to a close, there was dead silence in the huge hall. For a full fifteen seconds, not a sound could be heard. It was as though the law students and the assembled audience were digesting Kennedy's words, looking around nervously at their neighbors to test their reactions. Then, suddenly, surprisingly, a wave of applause rumbled through the room. People leaped to their feet and gave Kennedy a standing ovation.

the room. People leaped to their feet and gave Kennedy a standing ovation. He had survived his first crucial public encounter.

The very next week, the stirring rhetoric of the Law Day speech was put to the test. A group of civil rights activists, both white and black, had decided to challenge one of the most visible and cherished practices of Southern society: the separation of the races on buses and in bus terminals. Calling themselves Freedom Riders, they set out on a daring journey across the Deep South. Wherever they went, they broke the law—that is, they deliberately disobeyed the racist laws requiring that blacks and whites be segregated in public transportation.

Outraged whites met the Freedom Riders with protest and violence. Angry mobs descended on bus stations, jeering at the riders and eventually attacking them with fists and clubs. In Anniston, Alabama, a Greyhound bus was surrounded, then set on fire. Meanwhile, local and state police turned their backs, either pretending the situation did not exist or sometimes even helping the attackers.

Although they did not enjoy being attacked, the Freedom Riders had expected, and indeed even hoped, that their action would provoke a violent response. Photographs and news stories of the events flashed across the front pages of newspapers around the country, calling attention to the brutality of racism. Change, they believed, could only occur if the American people truly understood the depth of the ugliness abroad in the land.

In Washington, Robert Kennedy was caught by surprise. He had not known in advance about the Freedom Riders' plans, and now they presented a tricky problem. In a strictly legal sense, they were not his concern at all. Protection of people from violence is primarily a local and state matter, not the responsibility of the U.S. government. Yet, in this case, the local authorities were clearly subverting the law. In addition, because they were traveling from state to state, the Freedom Riders had in some ways an entitlement to federal protection.

Kennedy started by sending one of his top assistants, John Siegenthaler,

A bus carrying an interracial group of Freedom Riders was set on fire and destroyed in Anniston, Alabama. LIBRARY OF CONGRESS

to the South, to see if he could help defuse the situation. The Freedom Riders were due to arrive in Birmingham, Alabama, and Siegenthaler went to the bus station there to meet them and provide support. But a huge mob of angry whites was also there to greet the bus, and Siegenthaler, caught in the riot that ensued, was clubbed and ended up in the hospital. Hearing the news, Bobby Kennedy was furious. The public situation had suddenly become personal.

Meanwhile, the Freedom Riders were stuck in Birmingham. After the events of the day, the Greyhound bus company decided that it had had enough, and its officials refused to take the riders any farther. The attorney general of the United States found himself in the position of go-between, trying to arrange a ride to Mississippi for a ragtag, courageous, committed group of young people.

Kennedy personally contacted the bus company, demanding that it provide service to the riders. Not knowing the name of the supervisor he was speaking with, Kennedy simply called him Mr. Greyhound.

"Drivers refuse to drive the bus," the supervisor said.

"Do *you* know how to drive a bus?" Kennedy asked pointedly.

"No," the supervisor insisted.

"Well, surely somebody in the damn bus company can drive a bus, can't they?" Robert Kennedy burst out. "Somebody better get in the damn bus and get it going and get these people on their way."[4]

Mr. Greyhound managed to find a driver.

Kennedy's job was not over. He conducted negotiations with the governor of Alabama, trying with only partial success to convince him to provide protection for the riders. He sent federal marshals to Birmingham to help disperse a crowd that had trapped a group of blacks, including Dr. Martin Luther King Jr., in a church.

At the same time, he tried to convince the Freedom Riders themselves to put off the rest of their trip. Their point, he told them, had been made. Why ask for further trouble? Most of them went on anyway, to Jackson, Mississippi, where they ended up in jail for violating the law.

Although he wasn't beaten and pummeled, the Freedom Riders' journey took a great toll on Bobby Kennedy. Several sleepless nights left him haggard, and the complexities of his job were brought home to him. He had begun to make enemies. Even though he had offered some federal support, civil rights activists felt that he had not done nearly enough to stop the violence. On the other hand, even though he had not used federal force, Southern whites were outraged at the modest interventions that the Justice Department had made. As one Mississippi housewife said, speaking about the president of the United States, "Kennedy has too many brothers."[5]

Nevertheless, shortly after the Freedom Riders' journey, Bobby worked with another agency to change federal law. In September 1961, the Interstate Commerce Commission formally banned segregation in interstate bus terminals.

Although other major issues preoccupied Robert Kennedy during 1961 and 1962, civil rights remained a central concern. Kennedy was particularly sensitive, as many of his countrymen were not, to the connections between race and poverty in the United States. A number of people, even civil rights activists, felt that African Americans should concentrate on ending *legal* discrimination—the laws that kept blacks from voting or sitting side by side with whites in schools and universities. Bobby Kennedy understood, however, that there would be no long-term solution to the problem of race unless the nation took account of the fact that discrimination had also forced many blacks into poverty.

Kennedy was concerned, for example, about juvenile delinquency. The Justice Department was best set up to *react to* cases once they reached the court—but Kennedy was not content to wait. Instead, he redefined his department's mission and set in motion a series of programs designed to combat the root causes of crime. Rather than waiting for young people to show up in court, the government, Kennedy believed, should address their needs before they got into trouble.

Kennedy loved to tour the city schools in the District of Columbia, where the student population was predominantly African American. Often, he would take with him a well-known black entertainer, like singer Nat King Cole, or a football star like Bobby Mitchell of the Washington Redskins. He liked to challenge the young students to answer questions about American history: "How many of you know the names of the two generals who led the Union and Confederate armies at Gettysburg?" Or, "How many of you know who drafted the Bill of Rights?"[6] Kennedy's relaxed manner would encourage students to respond. He used the power of his office to raise money to support summer jobs for young Washingtonians, and each year on Christmas Day, he even opened up the Justice Department to sponsor a party for them.

Movie star Cary Grant accompanies Bobby on a tour of Washington, D.C., schools.
JOHN F. KENNEDY LIBRARY

Experiences in the field led to major policy initiatives. The President's Commission on Juvenile Delinquency was born in the Justice Department. So was the organizing effort behind the creation of VISTA—Volunteers in Service to America—a program that helped Americans become volunteers in the fight against poverty in the United States.

Over the next eighteen months, after the crisis of the Freedom Riders, there were few dramatic events in civil rights. Indeed, the hesitancy of the government to commit to action angered some civil rights leaders. John Kennedy, for example, had promised to end discrimination in federal housing by executive order, "the stroke of a pen," while he was on the campaign trail. But as president, he found that he did not want to offend

Southern senators in the Democratic Party, so he stalled on taking any public measures.

In the fall of 1962, however, events forced the Kennedy brothers to action. It was then that a young man named James Meredith was preparing to enroll in college. The problem, however, was that James Meredith was African American, and the college he wished to attend was the University of Mississippi, which had never (knowingly) admitted a black person in its entire history.

Meredith had followed, to the letter, the course that Robert Kennedy had prescribed in his Law Day speech. When his application was rejected because of his race, he took the university to court—and he won. A federal judge ordered the university to let Meredith enroll. It was clear, however, that state and university officials were prepared to make it very difficult for Meredith—perhaps, even, to ignore an order from a United States District Court.

The key figure in Mississippi was its governor, Ross Barnett, a whiny, wheedling man who prided himself on his loyalty to the people of his state. Barnett felt himself in a bind. He knew that if it came down to a contest between the state and the U.S. government, the U.S. would win. But he felt that he had to put up a fight, or else he would lose respect in the eyes of the white Mississippi voters who had elected him to office.

During the week before Meredith's scheduled registration, Bobby Kennedy and Ross Barnett played a cat-and-mouse game by telephone.

"You don't want to physically keep him out," Kennedy tried to persuade Barnett. "Governor, you are a part of the United States."

"We have been a part of the United States," Barnett complained, "but I don't know whether we are or not."

"Are you getting out of the Union?"

"It looks like we're getting kicked around—like we don't belong to it," replied the governor. "General, this thing is serious."

"It's serious here," Kennedy grimly concluded.[7]

Barnett, sensing defeat, tried to convince Kennedy to go along with a charade. He wanted the attorney general to send in federal marshals who would escort Meredith to campus. These marshals would draw their guns and make a show of force. The governor would then step aside and tell the people of his state that although he had done his best to stop the feds, he had had to give way in the face of overwhelming force. Failing that, Barnett proposed that the marshals should "sneak" Meredith onto campus and register him in secret. Again, he would be able to explain to Mississippians that the sneaky feds had done the deed behind his back.

Robert Kennedy wanted nothing of those proposals. He knew that to send in federal troops would further enrage bigots in the South. Nevertheless, he sat down with top military officials and prepared a careful plan, should troops become necessary.

On September 29, 1962, Meredith and a small cadre of federal marshals arrived in Oxford. For a full day, Barnett and university officials obstructed them at every turn, while continuing to negotiate with both Robert and John Kennedy by telephone. The Kennedys agreed to postpone the registration until the next day, Sunday, when there would be fewer people on campus.

The Sunday registration looked as though it would work. Even Barnett was caving in, though Robert Kennedy had to threaten to expose the governor's pretense on national television. Meredith arrived on campus, was spirited into a back room, and then was taken to a college dormitory. President Kennedy went on television to give a grand and stirring address about the triumph of law and order over the tide of discrimination.

Even as John Kennedy was delivering his talk from the East Room of the White House, bedlam was breaking loose in Oxford, Mississippi. For though Ross Barnett had reluctantly agreed to cooperate, the wave of hatred that he had helped to create was spilling onto the streets. From all over Mississippi, hundreds of angry whites had descended upon Oxford, and as day gave way to evening, their pent-up anger exploded. They surrounded the federal marshals, shouting ugly epithets. Rocks, bricks, and bottles filled the air. Gunshots rang out. A full-fledged riot erupted on the streets of the college town. The state and local police "mysteriously" vanished, and the marshals, along with James Meredith and two of Robert Kennedy's deputies, were left to fend for themselves.

Back in Washington, Robert and John Kennedy huddled with their top aides in the "situation room," the White House room designed to be the command center at a time of war. The situation in Oxford had turned into a domestic battle, and as the evening went on, it became clear that only one choice remained. The call went out to bring in the army.

By dawn, 20,000 federal troops rolled into Oxford, dispersing the crowd and restoring order. It was indeed the last resort—but once the bricks and bullets flew, the government had had little choice. James Meredith registered for college the next morning.

The Mississippi crisis, then, ended in victory, but again, the price was

James Meredith (center), accompanied by two U.S. marshals, registers at the University of Mississippi. LIBRARY OF CONGRESS

high. The stakes had been raised in the civil rights battle. Both sides were digging in. But now, at least, Robert Kennedy had demonstrated to the country that when the stakes were high, he was willing to use the full power of the federal government on behalf of the side of justice.

Victories like those of James Meredith were not coming fast enough for the African American community. The process was slow and frustrating. After all, blacks were simply asking for basic American rights—freedom of movement, choice in education, freedom from violence. Why, leaders like Martin Luther King Jr. were asking, should they have to wait? Why should they have to endure a lengthy and costly legal battle for each step forward? How many lives would be lost before equality under the law was a reality? Some of this frustration was directed at Robert Kennedy's Justice Department, which many people felt was not moving quickly enough in the right direction.

In the spring of 1963, some of this frustration became more public. Civil rights leaders organized a series of events in Birmingham, Alabama, where the Freedom Riders had been attacked two years earlier. On May 2, thousands of black schoolchildren marched through the streets of Birmingham, courageously putting themselves on the line to speak out for freedom. "Well, I don't approve of that. It's a bad thing to have children marching," Bobby Kennedy said privately. He was concerned that young people would be hurt.[8]

On May 3, civil rights leaders organized a second Birmingham march. This time, the outgoing police commissioner, an outspoken white supremacist named Bull Connor, ordered that dogs and fire hoses be turned on the marchers. Jets of water slammed against the demonstrators, flinging them against buildings and tossing them down the streets. German shepherds howled, lunged, and sank their teeth into unarmed men, women, and children.

The next day, photographs of the brutal response flashed across the country. Once again, Americans saw a clear picture of what their black countrymen were forced to suffer.

And again, Robert Kennedy intervened, sending two of his top assistants, Burke Marshall and Joseph Dolan, to Birmingham. There they helped negotiate a settlement that pushed Bull Connor out of office and ended some of the more blatant practices of discrimination in the city. But violence still spilled over. Martin Luther King Jr.'s brother's house was bombed; angry blacks retaliated with undisciplined rioting and looting. Tempers continued to flare.

In the wake of Birmingham, Robert Kennedy received a face-to-face taste of black frustration. He had asked the well-known writer James Baldwin to set up a meeting in New York City, where he could talk with some leading thinkers about the problems of black America, especially in the cities of the North. A dozen people converged on the Kennedy family apartment in Manhattan on May 24, 1963, to talk things over with the attorney general. Among those present were Baldwin, the playwright Lorraine Hansberry (*A Raisin in the Sun*), singers Lena Horne and Harry Belafonte, and psychologist Kenneth Clark, who would soon publish a major study called *Dark Ghetto*.

The meeting, however, was dominated not by these major figures but by a young activist named Jerome Smith. Smith had been a Freedom Rider, and later, he worked with the Congress on Racial Equality (CORE), one of the most important civil rights organizations. Committed to peaceful civil disobedience, he had spent many months in jail over the last few years.

Smith began the meeting in the Central Park West apartment by telling Kennedy, "I want you to understand that I don't care anything about you or your brother." He was "nauseated," he said, that it was necessary for him to be there. Some of the other people in the room understood and sympathized with what Smith meant. It was upsetting, even sickening, for African Americans to be so oppressed in their own country that they had to come and explain their predicament to one of the senior members of the U.S. government. Bobby Kennedy, however, thought that Smith was talking about him. The conversation was already off on the wrong foot.

Smith continued in a lengthy, emotional monologue. He talked about his experiences as an activist. At the beginning, he said, he had been fully committed to nonviolence—but after years of suffering, he now felt himself tempted to take more forceful action. "When I pull the trigger," he said, "kiss it good-bye." No, he said, in answer to a question, he could never, never, never fight on behalf of his country.

Few in the room agreed with everything that Smith said. Some, indeed, like Kenneth Clark, had come prepared to talk about more specific ideas for change. But the other black leaders felt that it was important for Kennedy to hear Smith's rage, so they allowed the young man to dominate the meeting.

As the conversation continued, Kennedy became more tense, the blacks in the room more heated. They attacked his slow response in Mississippi and Birmingham, they railed against the viciousness of the FBI, and they rejected the attorney general's claims that he had worked closely with Martin Luther King Jr.

Kennedy predicted that a Negro would be elected president within forty years. After all, he told them, his family had suffered discrimination as Irish Americans, but now, two generations later, his brother was president of the United States. That prompted James Baldwin to complain, "Your family has been here for three generations. My family has been here far longer than that. Why is your brother at the top while we are still so far away?"

For three hours, the meeting went on, and Kennedy came away exhausted and discouraged. In a sense, the day had been typical of his situation as attorney general. In the morning, he had negotiated with the owners of department stores, trying to convince them to desegregate their lunch counters in the South. Those powerful whites hated and distrusted Kennedy's interference in their business affairs. In the afternoon, he had found himself the target of attack from blacks, who argued that he was not doing enough to advance their cause.[9]

Kennedy also found himself in a dilemma involving the country's most eloquent civil rights leader, Dr. Martin Luther King Jr. In 1960, Kennedy

Dr. Martin Luther King Jr. often urged Bobby to use the power of the federal government to enforce civil rights for African Americans.
LIBRARY OF CONGRESS

had helped get King out of jail. Now, as attorney general, he relied on King's advice and cooperation.

During the same period, however, the FBI had been conducting its own investigations of civil rights organizations—targeting Martin Luther King in particular. Like Joseph McCarthy ten years before, J. Edgar Hoover was on the lookout for Communists everywhere. Hoover believed that Communists had infiltrated the civil rights leadership and were using black discontent to help bring about a revolution in the U.S. The idea was preposterous. But Hoover did manage to establish that some of King's associates had at one time had *some* association with the Communist Party, and he blew these links all out of proportion to make his point.

For a long time, Robert Kennedy managed to brush aside Hoover's charges, but by mid-1963, the FBI director's persistent attempts paid off. Kennedy did not genuinely believe that Martin Luther King was a threat to national security. But Hoover's slim evidence convinced the attorney general that the *appearance* of Communist influence could be a political liability, not just for King but for the Kennedy administration.

Worried that public fears about Communism could wipe out civil rights gains, Kennedy made a serious error in judgment. He gave the FBI permission to upgrade its investigation of King to include wiretaps on his telephone and his residence.

The full details of this activity did not come out until years after the deaths of both Kennedy and King, but it eventually became clear that Kennedy had participated in a gross abuse of government power. He had envisioned a limited investigation, with a limited scope. But the FBI took the ball and ran with it, taking the attorney general's narrow permission for wiretaps as unofficial license to gather information on every aspect of King's private life, as well as his public connections. Kennedy never knew the full extent of the FBI's actions. Nevertheless, his approval was an ugly counterbalance to an otherwise distinguished record of championing the cause of justice and freedom for African Americans.

The events of the previous years had solidified Kennedy's overall commitment to the civil rights cause. He still believed in process, but his own temperament was fervent. By 1963, he could appreciate more fully the force of the feeling that underlay the African American yearning for freedom and equality. He did not brush off events like the heated conversation with James Baldwin and others in New York. He absorbed even the difficult moments into his complex approach to a major national issue.

With his leadership, the Justice Department had gone further than ever before—not just in upholding the law, but in working to change it to better serve the cause of justice. The culminating triumph would come in 1964, with the passage of the most sweeping civil rights act in American history. This measure ended many of the most blatant discriminatory practices in the United States. It ended segregation in many public facilities, struck down laws designed to prevent blacks from voting, and reaffirmed the federal government's commitment to equality.

Civil rights protests were not limited to the South. In Boston, African Americans lobbied for equal educational opportunities. BOSTON PUBLIC LIBRARY

Strong as this law was, however, Robert Kennedy knew that it would not be enough. As he had understood in 1961 when he met with the gangs in Harlem, racial discrimination in American life could not be undone simply through legislation. Deep problems—enduring prejudice, the rut of poverty, unequal access to education and housing—lay just below the surface. These problems could not simply be solved in Washington. They had to be attacked—day by day, case by case—on rural Southern back roads and on the streets of American cities.

chapter five

"Why, God?"
The JFK Assassination and
Its Aftermath

(1963–1967)

How dull it is to pause, to make an end,
To rust unburnished, not to shine in use!

John Fitzgerald Kennedy treated his vice president, Lyndon Baines Johnson, fairly, even generously. In Johnson's words, JFK gave him "dignity and standing," but inevitably, the president turned to his brother for advice. "Don't kid anybody about who is the top adviser," Johnson said. "Bobby is first in, last out. Bobby is the boy he listens to." In Johnson's eyes, Bobby had usurped his rightful position. JFK should have turned to him.[1]

"Every time I came into John Kennedy's presence, I felt like a goddamn raven hovering over his shoulder," Johnson said. In his mind, he had been reduced to a bird of ill omen, a messenger bird flapping his wings to remind the president of his mortality, fluttering within reach in case something monstrous happened. One day it did.

November 22, 1963, was uncommonly warm—and the attorney general was poolside at Hickory Hill with Ethel and two associates. On a lunch break from a meeting on organized crime, they were eating tuna sandwiches and sipping cups of clam chowder.

Ethel answered the extension phone at about 1:30 P.M. and handed it to her husband. "J. Edgar Hoover," she said. The attorney general was surprised. Why would Hoover call me here? he wondered. There must be something wrong.

"I have news for you," said the FBI director. "The president's been shot . . . I think it's serious." Hoover's voice was cold and distant.

Bobby clapped his hand over his mouth. Seeing his face twist with horror, Ethel rushed toward him. He tried to force the words out. In a few seconds, he murmured, "Jack's been shot. It may be fatal."

Bobby struggled to regain his composure. He telephoned the president's party at the Parkland Hospital in Dallas. "How serious is it?" Bobby asked. "Is he conscious? Has anyone sent for a priest? Please call me back." Bobby worried about Jackie. He worried about the competence of doctors who were attending to his brother.

He charged up the steps to change his clothes. He intended to rush to Dallas to be at his brother's side. Captain Tazwell "Taz" Shepard, White House staff member and naval aide to President Kennedy, called Bobby back. "The president is dead," he said.

Bobby tried to piece the story together. The president's plane had landed in Dallas, Texas, at 11:30 A.M. (Central Standard Time). Ten minutes later, he and Jackie were in a motorcade en route to downtown Dallas, where he was scheduled to speak at an annual meeting of the Citizens Council at the Trade Mart.

The president and Jackie were sitting in the back of an open bubble-top limousine, greeting admiring crowds and talking to Governor and Mrs. John B. Connally, who were in the front seat. Thousands of Texans along the route cheered the president.

At 12:30 P.M., shots rang out. The president and Governor Connally were hit and rushed to emergency rooms at Parkland Hospital. The First Lady and Mrs. Connally escaped injury.

Bobby made frantic calls to his mother and his brother and sisters. He offered them comfort and direction. He talked to Eunice, who said she would go to their mother in Hyannisport. He asked Sargent Shriver, Eunice's husband, to handle the funeral arrangements. He asked Teddy to tend to their father.

Friends arrived at Hickory Hill to try to comfort Bobby, among them David Hackett and Edwin Guthman. On a walk with Ed Guthman, Bobby said, "There's so much bitterness. I thought they'd get one of us, but Jack, after all he'd been through, never worried about it. . . . I thought it would be me."[2]

Less than two hours after President Kennedy's assassination, Lyndon Baines Johnson was sworn in as president on board the plane that carried the former president's body back to Washington. Jackie was at Lyndon Johnson's side. The plane landed at Andrews Air Force Base shortly after 6:00 P.M.

Bobby arrived a half hour earlier. Alone, he paced in the darkness. Then, he sat limp for a few moments in the back of an abandoned military truck. When Air Force One landed, he darted to the front entrance of the plane and down the aisle past Lyndon Baines Johnson to Jackie. Johnson interpreted Bobby's rush past him as a deliberate snub.

Bobby saw his brother's blood on Jackie's clothes and stockings. He clasped her hands. "Oh, Bobby," she cried. He put his arms around her. Bobby and Jackie accompanied the president's bronze coffin to Bethesda Naval Hospital. "I just can't believe Jack has gone," Jackie whispered.[3]

Bobby appeared contained, but as he listened to his sister-in-law describe what she had endured, he brought to the surface every ounce of courage that he possessed.

After a brief, fitful sleep, Bobby stopped by the Oval Office, where he was struck by the half-filled crates of his brother's belongings. The reality of the assassination overwhelmed him.

When the new chief executive approached him in the Oval Office, Bobby raised his arms in an effort to block LBJ's entrance to the dismantled room. "You can't come in here," he screamed. "You don't have any business in here. Don't come in here!"

LBJ was stunned. "You're making a big mistake," he answered. "I'm the president of the United States, and you have no business in any way to interfere with my constitutional duties." LBJ tried to explain to Bobby why he needed to move into the Oval Office so quickly: Dean Rusk and Robert McNamara had insisted he do so in order to create the appearance of a smooth transition to office.

Bobby's voice grew even more shrill. "You should not be here! You don't deserve to be here."

On that same morning, the slain president's flag-draped casket was placed on a catafalque in the East Room. Bobby appeared controlled. He attended to countless decisions: What should be done with Jack's personal belongings? Where should his brother be buried? Should the casket be left open or closed? But late that night, when he entered the stately Lincoln bedroom and closed the door, Bobby bent his head and in a torrent of emotion sobbed, "Why, God? Why?" He could find no reason, no explanation, no justification for his brother's death.[4]

Bobby's bitter relationship with Lyndon Baines Johnson had begun at the 1960 Democratic National Convention in Los Angeles. When John Fitzgerald Kennedy captured the presidential nomination on the first ballot, he invited the former Senate majority leader to be his vice-presidential running mate. Jack Kennedy thought the shrewd Texas politician would assure his victory, but he also worried that liberal convention delegates might not agree.

At his brother's urging, Bobby visited Johnson in his hotel suite to ask if he would be willing to withdraw his name if things got too rough on the convention floor.

Bobby unwittingly awakened in the rangy Texan a deep-rooted fear of rejection and humiliation. Johnson's face contorted and his eyes brimmed with tears. More than anything in the world, Johnson wanted the nomination, and he believed that Bobby was trying to destroy his political career.

Bobby, in turn, was riled at Johnson for several reasons. Johnson had been against President Kennedy's policy in Cuba. He took issue on other foreign policy matters but offered no alternative solutions. He did little to solve political strife in his home state of Texas. At meetings, he seemed reluctant to share his opinions and was often silent, his face empty of expression. And now, he had moved into the White House with unconscionable swiftness.

Johnson had been born in a modest farmhouse on the banks of the Pedernales River in Texas. He had a vision of his own for America, which he would call the Great Society, but he was also suspicious, given to petty thinking and insecurities. He was confused and threatened by Bobby Kennedy.

LBJ quickly aligned himself with J. Edgar Hoover, Bobby's nemesis at the

Jackie and Bobby Kennedy at the funeral of President John F. Kennedy JOHN F. KENNEDY LIBRARY

FBI. For the nine months that Bobby would remain as attorney general, J. Edgar Hoover never said to Bobby that he was sorry about his brother's death. Hoover fed Johnson's insecurities by hinting that Bobby was leading a conspiracy to oust Johnson from the 1964 presidential ticket so that Bobby could become president.

For months after his brother's murder, grief held Bobby in its iron grip. His face was ashen, his eyes swollen and rimmed with red. Other people close to him had died—his brother Joe Jr. and his sister Kick, and he had mourned their deaths—but there was something more charged about the loss of Jack.

Bobby lost his appetite and vitality. His clothes began to hang loosely on his body. He took long walks alone or with Brumus lapping at his heels. Ethel, usually able to coax her husband out of melancholy, could do nothing.

Bobby entered realms he had never traveled—tumultuous storms of uncertainty, ambiguity, and anguish. He and his brother had shared a vision for America. He worried that their high hopes and aspirations would recede, never to be realized. What could he do alone? What would become of him? How could he go forward?

The attorney general felt the crushing blow to himself, but he also sensed something larger, more profound—the colossal and tragic loss to the nation. In office for only a thousand days, Jack had inspired hope. His presidency had held out new and exciting expectations and possibilities.

Bobby's mind cast backward into the pathways of memory, to the stories Jack told him as a boy, to laughter that filled the house when Jack came home from school, to his mother's admonitions, to his dad's cries to win, win, win. The brothers' lives had become intertwined like the roots of a tree.

Bobby became more reflective than he had ever been. He read the Greek playwrights Aeschylus and Sophocles and found comfort in their words. He trusted these ancient sages, and he memorized lines from their plays. He read over and over again a copy of Edith Hamilton's *The Greek Way* that Jackie had given him. He also immersed himself in the works of George Bernard Shaw, Albert Camus, and Ralph Waldo Emerson.

Bobby started wearing Jack's tattered tweed overcoat. He often left the coat behind and sent an aide to retrieve it, just as Jack had done. He started smoking the small cigars that Jack enjoyed smoking. He often quoted his brother. He displayed many of his brother's memorabilia in his office.

Sorrow etched itself in deep furrows in his brow. Lines newly carved appeared around his mouth and eyes. His striking blue eyes appeared haunted, and he hunched forward, shoulders bent.

He made his first public speech after his brother's death in Scranton, Pennsylvania, on St. Patrick's Day, March 17, 1964, to the Friendly Sons of St. Patrick, a group of Irish Americans. He had accepted the invitation reluctantly. When his airplane landed at Scranton/Wilkes-Barre Airport, more than two thousand young people broke through barriers to catch a glimpse of Bobby and to touch him. Police had to clear a path for the attorney general.

Bobby was startled by the throng of ten thousand fans who lined the route to the new John F. Kennedy Elementary School—the first elementary school in the United States to be named after JFK—where he officiated at ground-breaking ceremonies. He then traveled on to the Hotel Casey, where he spoke.

On this occasion, Bobby honored his Irish roots and his slain brother. He realized, for the first time since Jack's death, that he was becoming recognized for his own accomplishments. He could make a difference in people's lives. Perhaps he could carry the Kennedy torch forward.

As Bobby began to inch out of despair, he wondered whether he should seek the vice presidency as Lyndon Johnson's running mate in the 1964 presidential election. As vice president, he could carry on his brother's work and nurture his own constituency, but there were problems, too. How loyal could he be to Lyndon Johnson? Could he ever take an independent position? Would President Johnson pay any attention to him?

As Bobby deliberated about his political future, misfortune struck the

Kennedy family again. On June 19, 1964, Edward Kennedy went down in a plane crash en route to a Massachusetts Democratic Convention in Springfield. The pilot and a Kennedy aide died instantly. Teddy and two others survived. Bobby rushed to his brother's side. Teddy, barely conscious, with a broken back, punctured lung, and massive internal bleeding, quipped to Bobby when he recognized him, "Is it true that you are ruthless?"[5]

In 1964, the rift between Bobby Kennedy and Lyndon Johnson grew deeper. Bobby was thirty-eight years old, Johnson fifty-five. Johnson was 6 feet 4 inches, rangy and sprawling; Bobby was 5 feet 10 inches, taut and wiry. Johnson was the oldest and best loved of five children from a poor family; Bobby was the seventh of nine children in a family of means. Bobby was obsessed by physical activity: football, skiing, sailing. Johnson was not. But they were divided by more than age or size or interests. Johnson mistrusted New England and Harvard intellectualism. Bobby mistrusted Texas bravado and largesse. Manliness for the Texas rancher involved the use of crude language and epithets.

In addition, Bobby was shy, a private person, restrained. Johnson was gregarious and rambling. Bobby sometimes said so little that people were awkward in his presence, whereas Johnson was a talker who liked to tell a rattlin' good tale.

In some ways, they were like two pesky schoolboys scrambling for a place on the team, but it went deeper than that. When LBJ balked at having him as a running mate, Bobby's future seemed clear for the first time since Jack's death: He would resign from his post as attorney general and run for the Senate in New York.

Johnson was still worried. Bobby was scheduled to deliver a tribute to his fallen brother at the Democratic convention in Atlantic City. Afraid that there might be a groundswell of support for Bobby, Johnson had the tribute shifted from Tuesday night to Thursday night. By then, a vice-presidential candidate would have already been named.

By Thursday, Johnson selected Minnesota Senator Hubert Humphrey as

Grief and long-simmering tensions made for a strained relationship between Bobby Kennedy and President Lyndon Johnson. LIBRARY OF CONGRESS, *LOOK* COLLECTION

his running mate. Bobby himself was preoccupied with the tribute to his brother. He was uneasy. He read over the manuscript introducing *A Thousand Days*, the film memorial of JFK's presidential years. He penciled in a few changes.

Senator Henry "Scoop" Jackson of Washington, presiding at the convention, called Bobby to the rostrum. Bobby was not prepared for what took place. As he stood at the microphone ready to begin, the audience stood in thunderous applause.

Bobby tried to start: "Mr. Chairman . . . Mr. Chairman . . . ," but the audience became a great roar refusing to subside. Bobby tried to control his own

welling emotion. He smiled timidly, tentatively, sadness mixed with grati-
tude. Repeatedly he tried to start: "Mr. Chairman . . . Mr. Chairman . . ."
Jackson leaned toward him, "Let it go on . . . Just let them do it, Bob," he
whispered. "Let them get it out of their systems." The ovation continued for
twenty-two minutes.[6]

Buoyed by the unforgettable support and affirmation, Bobby Kennedy
turned toward the Senate race in New York. He faced a tough opponent in
Kenneth Keating. He also faced cries of carpetbagging, since he had not
lived full-time in New York for many years. President Johnson campaigned
on his behalf. On the surface, he seemed earnest. "You don't often find a

Bobby Kennedy eulogizes his brother Jack at the Democratic National Convention. JOHN F.
KENNEDY LIBRARY

man," Johnson said, "who has the understanding, the heart and the compassion that Bobby Kennedy has." But underneath, Johnson was envious of the attention the crowds paid Bobby. He felt their outstretched hands should have been extended toward him.

Bobby won the election, defeating incumbent Senator Keating by 719,693 votes. Democrats Lyndon Johnson and Hubert Humphrey scored a whopping victory over Republicans Barry M. Goldwater and William E. Miller. They won the election by 15,000,000 votes, an unprecedented popular majority.

Bobby took the oath of office on January 4, 1965. His brother Teddy, his back in a steel brace, was sworn in at the same time. They were the first brothers to serve together in the Senate since 1803. Bobby appointed Adam Walinsky and Peter Edelman as his legislative assistants. His office became a whirlwind of activity. More than twelve hundred letters poured in daily.

As a freshman senator, he was at the bottom of the list in terms of seniority, and Senate protocol called for him to wait his turn to speak. It was a great reversal of fortune for the former number-two man in Washington, D.C.

He often turned to his brother for advice. Although younger, Teddy was the more senior senator. When trying to prompt action on a bill, Bobby asked, "What should I do now? You know how to handle these fellows . . . You're the likable one."

Still, Robert Kennedy's heart and soul were alive to people on the streets of America. He walked the ghettos of New York City, seeking those who didn't have money even for a cup of coffee. He talked to beggars and outcasts, explored the tenements and lodging houses. "Millions of people need help," he commented. "My God, they need help."

In Brooklyn, New York, nearly a half million people were crammed into the slum-ridden ghetto of Bedford-Stuyvesant. The predominantly black community was frustrated and angry. Bobby was horrified by the wretched state of poor people living behind boarded-up windows in condemned buildings and by drug addicts shooting up heroin in doorways.

He was appalled, too, by the statistics. Eighty percent of Bedford-

One of Bobby Kennedy's major initiatives while a U.S. senator was to revitalize the Bedford-Stuyvesant neighborhood in Brooklyn. NEW YORK TIMES

Stuyvesant children did not finish high school. The infant mortality rate was higher than anywhere else in the nation. Thirty percent of the population had annual incomes of less than three thousand dollars.

When Bobby met with members of the Bedford-Stuyvesant community, they lashed out at him. Thomas R. Jones, a black State Supreme Court Judge, said, "I'm weary of study, Senator . . . weary of speeches, weary of promises that aren't kept."[7]

Bobby was determined to do something about Bedford-Stuyvesant. He recommended that community leaders and residents form the Bedford-Stuyvesant Restoration Corporation. The Restoration Corporation's main charge was to determine exactly what was needed.

He recommended, too, the formation of the Bedford-Stuyvesant Development and Services Corporation, to be made up of business leaders. He recruited heads from such corporations as IBM (International Business Machines) and CBS (Columbia Broadcasting System). The function of the Development and Services Corporation was to raise funds and to advise.

"If I could do what I really wanted to do," Bobby said, "I would resign from the Senate and run Bedford-Stuyvesant." Bobby took pride in the project. He believed in the vitality of local planning and community action. He believed in the importance of residents' feeling good about their neighborhood.

Bobby's commitment to Bedford-Stuyvesant paid off. Houses were built and refurbished, and parks were designed. Small businesses owned by black merchants sprang up. Recreational and cultural services became available.

The plight of Native Americans in the United States also stirred Bobby. He visited poverty-stricken reservations and talked to Indians. He was concerned about the 76 percent dropout rate among Indian schoolchildren forced by the U.S. government to attend boarding schools, often thousands of miles from their homes. He was appalled at the number of newborn infants who died needlessly because of poor health care. He believed that Native Americans were victims of discrimination in their own land.

He became more and more closely identified with the poor and disenfranchised. Violence, poverty, civil rights, and the suffering of the masses took the place of his old enemies, organized crime and Communism. He also became closely identified with children. His senate staff worked on projects for new playgrounds and school lunch programs. He was relaxed with children.

Bobby took up other causes. In the Senate, Bobby cosponsored an amendment with Republican Senator Jacob Javits that enabled 100,000 Puerto Ricans to vote. His amendment to extend Appalachian antipoverty aid to

New York passed. He worked hard to curb firearm shipments between states and to curb cigarette advertisements.

In March 1965, his ongoing obsession with physical activity led him to embark on a mission to become the first person to climb a mountain in Canada that had recently been named for his slain brother. Mount Kennedy was 13,880 feet high and four miles inside the Canadian border in the Yukon Territory. The adventure was sponsored by the National Geographic Society.

James W. Whittaker, the mission's leader, a man of vast climbing experience who had climbed Mount Everest, requested Bobby's vital statistics so he could gather appropriate gear. When Whittaker met Kennedy in person, he worried because Bobby looked tired and out of shape. "What have you

The climb up Mount Kennedy in the Yukon Territory in Canada was both a physical challenge and a personal triumph for Bobby. SPORTS ILLUSTRATED

done to get into condition?" Whittaker inquired. "I've run up and down the stairs at home and practiced hollering 'help.'"[8]

Bobby Kennedy had little understanding that the word *help* might really be necessary. He had no knowledge of the use of ice axes or the eccentricities of weather—breathtaking cold, biting winds, icy storms that brought everything to a halt.

The climb was far more treacherous than Bobby expected. As he approached a terrifying vertical wall of ice, he worried that he might not make it. Even seasoned climbers like Whittaker sensed the danger. Bobby was tied by rope to Whittaker and climber Barry Prather for safety. Still, if he fell, he knew he would hang precariously over a three-thousand-foot cliff until they reeled him in. He pitched upward, staving off the panic and illusory pull from the steep wall.

Bobby climbed the last sixty feet to the summit alone. He knelt down and made the sign of the cross. He carved a hole in the ice and placed in it symbols of his martyred brother's New Frontier: a copy of the late president's 1961 inaugural address, a PT-109 tie clip, and a newly minted Kennedy half-dollar.

He raised the flag he had brought bearing the Kennedy family crest. It was an exhilarating experience for him to be the first person to reach the summit of the high mountain named in honor of his brother. It felt good. It was a catharsis, a cleansing of the soul. "I'm glad that I did it," he said, "and I'm glad that it's over."[9]

But it was clearly not only physical challenges that occupied the New York senator. In the fall of 1965, he embarked on a trip to South America (Chile, Argentina, Brazil), where he was instinctively drawn to the barrios and favelas, the shacks built on the outskirts of cities. He lifted barefoot children in his arms, and he greeted occupants of makeshift shelters.

"It's outrageous," he exclaimed. "Those people are living like animals, and the children—the children don't have a chance. What happened to all our AID money? Where is it going? Wouldn't you be a Communist if you had to live there?" he said to Richard Goodwin, Kennedy friend, supporter, and speechwriter. "I would," he added.[10]

On Bobby's visit to South Africa, he met with residents of the segregated black community of Soweto. JOHN F. KENNEDY LIBRARY

Bobby's global concerns also included South Africa. He was against South Africa's policy of apartheid, which kept blacks and whites separated and denied blacks any share of political or economic power.

South African blacks could not buy land; they could not attend the church of their choice; husbands were forced to ask official permission to live with their families. When Bobby received an invitation from an antiapartheid student group, the National Union of South African Students (NUSAS), to speak at its yearly Day of Affirmation, he accepted.

But the trip had the makings of a disaster. The pro-apartheid South African government was afraid Bobby would stir up trouble. Furious at Ian Robertson of NUSAS for inviting Bobby, the South African government barred Robertson from political and social life for five years. It took them five months to issue Bobby a visa.

It became a politically explosive situation. When the Kennedy party—which included Bobby; Ethel; Angie Novello, his secretary; and Adam Walinsky, aide and speechwriter—landed at Johannesburg, more than fifteen hundred people greeted them. Bobby seemed on edge. Some screamed, "Yankee go home." Others roared their enthusiasm.

The day after his arrival, Bobby paid a special visit to Ian Robertson in political exile on a remote island (Robben Island). In the evening, Bobby made the trip to the University of Cape Town to deliver the Day of Affirmation speech. It contained his deepest and most profound belief.

At the university, Bobby said, "Each time a man stands up for an ideal, or acts to improve the lot of others, or strikes out against injustice, he sends forth a tiny ripple of hope, and crossing each other from a million different centers of energy and daring, those ripples build a current which can sweep down the mightiest walls of oppression and resistance." The crowd erupted in loud applause.

His words were spoken in a far more persuasive way than ever before. His voice seemed deeper, more sonorous. His pacing was far better, his pauses and inflections thoughtful and effective, his passion discernible. The talk conveyed his capacity not only to identify with the powerless and the dispossessed but to inspire them.

Death remained a cruel intruder in Bobby's life. In September 1966, Ethel's brother, George Skakel, and Bobby's Harvard friend, Dean Markham, died in a plane crash. "You had better pretend you don't know me," he said to Ted Sorensen. "Everyone connected with me seems jinxed."[11]

At times after his brother Jack's death, Bobby wavered in his belief in God. "One question which really shakes me, really shakes me—if God exists why do poor people exist? Why does a Hitler arise? I can't give an answer for that. Only faith . . . Religion is a salve for confusion and misdirection." He believed in God because he chose to believe.[12]

Also occupying the senator was Vietnam, a narrow spit of land on the Gulf of Tonkin and the South China Sea, with rugged mountains and serpentine rivers that loop and bend through miles of rich delta. South Vietnam was fighting a war against the Communists in North Vietnam—and the U.S. was assisting the South Vietnamese.

LBJ believed that if he let the Communists take over South Vietnam, he would be viewed as a coward and the United States would be seen as an appeaser. He worried about Bobby Kennedy's reaction. "There would be Robert Kennedy leading the fight against me, telling everyone that I had betrayed John Kennedy's commitment to South Vietnam. That I had let a democracy fall into the hands of the Communists. That I was a coward. An unmanly man. A man without a spine."[13]

And, in truth, perhaps for the first time, he now had something to fear from Bobby, but not for the reasons he thought.

As he watched the body bag count escalate, the senator's position on Vietnam began to change. Bobby began to speak out against the war and to press for a negotiated settlement.

Bobby badgered Johnson to stop the heavy bombing in North Vietnam and to involve the National Liberation Front, the political arm of the Vietcong, in peace talks. Vice President Hubert Humphrey likened Bobby's thinking to letting "a fox in the chicken coop." Bobby became convinced that any time he openly opposed the war, it toughened Johnson's policies in Vietnam.

In March 1967, he told the Senate: "Three presidents have taken action in Vietnam. As one who was involved in many of those decisions, I can testify that if fault is to be found or responsibility assessed, there is enough to go around for all, including myself." He no longer believed that America could resolve every single problem that existed in the world.[14]

After months, even years, of mourning, Bobby's grief had transformed itself into a clamoring call to idealism. The earnestness was still there, and the passion had returned. He had the commitment; the concern over Vietnam, poverty, and racial injustice; the sensitivity to the needs of individuals in the nooks, eddies, and ghettos of Harlem and Bedford-Stuyvesant and in the barrios of South America.

There was also something else—the first stirrings of the 1968 presidential campaign.

chapter six

The Last Campaign
(1968)

The lights begin to twinkle from the rocks;
The long day wanes; the slow moon climbs; the deep
Moans round with many voices. Come, my friends,
'Tis not too late to seek a newer world.

At the start of 1968, the United States faced escalating problems: poverty, racial tensions, violence, the war in Vietnam. It was a frenzied, pulsating, bizarre time in the history of the nation.

As the new year dawned, 100,000 American soldiers, many of them boys of eighteen and nineteen, had been wounded in Vietnam. Almost 16,000 had lost their lives. The horror of the war could no longer be swept under the rug.

At home, Bobby Kennedy was under pressure to act. Those who hated the war in Vietnam were searching anxiously for a leader, for a national politician who would lead the fight against the bloodshed.

In 1960, Jack Kennedy had given Bobby a cigarette box as a gift for managing his presidential campaign. "When I'm through, how about you?" was the inscription. As a senator, Jack had said, "Just as I went into politics because Joe died, if anything happened to me tomorrow, my brother would run for my seat in the Senate. And if Bobby died, Teddy would take over for him."

Now Bobby's admirers were egging him on. Why didn't he challenge Lyndon Johnson for the 1968 Democratic presidential nomination? Their expectation was that someday Bobby would run for president. Why not now?

The senator asked himself several questions: Would running be viewed as a part of his bitter feud with Lyndon Johnson? Would the press say that he was motivated by arrogance? How would his stance as an antiwar Democrat play itself out? Bobby Kennedy was usually confident, decisive. But now he seemed uncertain.

He knew how much could be accomplished in the executive branch of government and he believed he could bring Americans back together again. But would he be smarter to wait until 1972 to run for office?

Although Bobby prized courage above all virtues, he was ensnared by fear. Incumbent presidents were almost impossible to beat. The last time a sitting president like Johnson had been denied renomination was in 1884. His brother Jack had depended on him to manage his presidential campaign and to champion his causes, but whom did Bobby have?

Yet, like a magnet, the 1968 presidential race pulled him closer to the fray. Television brought into people's homes the most horrifying photographs and film footage the nation had ever seen: the image of a grieving Vietnamese mother holding her dead child, the photo of a Vietnamese Buddhist monk on a Saigon street burning himself to death, photos of young American soldiers battered and ruined embracing each other in a war that was never formally declared.

When Senator Eugene McCarthy, the peace candidate from Minnesota, entered New Hampshire, the first presidential primary, Bobby was brought closer to throwing his own hat into the ring. Although both men were senators, Irish Catholics, and antiwar Democrats, there were striking differences in style. McCarthy was aloof, cerebral, distanced. Bobby was more one with the people. McCarthy was laid-back; Bobby worked like a beaver. But McCarthy's entry into the campaign alleviated some of Bobby's own fear about challenging Johnson.

Yet Bobby still held back. He was haunted by misgivings and insecurities. The polls had swung in Johnson's favor. He didn't think he could pull off a victory. On January 30, 1968, Bobby said to journalists, "I have told friends and supporters who are urging me to run that I would not oppose Lyndon Johnson under any foreseeable circumstances."[1]

Bobby's people took the statement as the final word. Several joined ranks with Eugene McCarthy, who had attracted students and idealists, many of whom were similar to Bobby's followers: people determined to stop the war in Vietnam. They felt convinced that nothing would draw Bobby into combat with Lyndon Johnson for the presidency.

And then not even twelve hours after he had made the announcement, the unforeseeable circumstance occurred. The Vietcong, North Vietnam's guerrilla army, launched a surprise offensive in Vietnam. On Tet, the Vietnamese New Year, soldiers attacked thirty South Vietnam towns and cities and assaulted airfields and military bases.

In a daring act, special Vietcong forces blasted their way through the massive ten-foot-high wall surrounding the American embassy in Saigon, the capital of South Vietnam. Embassy marine guards fought desperately against the invaders. The embassy was severely threatened. The American public was stunned and shaken.

President Johnson had led Americans to believe that victory in Vietnam was close at hand. In an effort to gain public confidence, he had issued promising reports. But this clearly was not victory. President Johnson had been trapped in his own web, and his popularity sagged.

Bobby Kennedy brooded. He was now convinced that Johnson would do nothing to end the conflict. If only he had waited before saying so definitely that he would *not* run for president.

"Our enemy, savagely striking at will across all of South Vietnam," he said in a speech in Chicago on February 4, 1968, "has finally shattered the mask of official illusion with which we have concealed our true circumstances even from ourselves . . ."[2]

Bobby now leaned toward running for the presidency. A week before the New Hampshire primary, talk in Bobby's inner circle shifted to campaign strategy. When should he announce? Where? How much support in the Democratic Party could he count on? Already he had missed deadlines for two primaries. He had to gear up quickly for the six remaining ones.

On March 10, 1968, Bobby attended a rally in Delano, California, in the San Joaquin Valley. He closely identified with "la Causa," the movement of

In 1968, the war in Vietnam was claiming thousands of American lives and sparking political controversy at home. BOSTON PUBLIC LIBRARY

striking farmworkers and their leader, Cesar Chavez. He was inspired by the Mexican American's determination on behalf of California's grape pickers. For twenty-five days, Chavez had endured a hunger strike to protest the exploitation of his people. Bobby joined Chavez for the breaking of the fast.[3]

In a small chapel, Bobby and Cesar Chavez met and walked arm in arm in a procession to the town square for a public mass. At Communion, the fast was broken when the Communion bread was shared. Chavez himself had worked in the vineyards from the time he was a boy. He had little formal education and little use for politicians. He was attracted to Mahatma Gandhi and Saint Francis. He was also attracted to Bobby Kennedy.

Bobby meets with Cesar Chavez at the conclusion of Chavez's hunger strike to protest working conditions of migrant workers. JOHN F. KENNEDY LIBRARY

Bobby, in turn, was compelled by Chavez's stamina and courage on behalf of his people. Bobby believed in Cesar Chavez's cause. Standing on top of a flatbed truck, Bobby addressed over six thousand farmworkers. "Viva la Causa! Viva Cesar Chavez!" his words rang out.

Two days later, Senator Eugene McCarthy scored a startling moral victory, winning 42 percent of the vote in the first presidential primary in New Hampshire. McCarthy's success showed that Johnson was vulnerable, and it threw the president's renomination into serious doubt.

The Tet offensive and McCarthy's strong showing destroyed Johnson's credibility and ended Bobby's reluctance to engage in head-to-head political combat. He would take on Lyndon Johnson and the war.

No longer victimized by his own inertia, he pitched himself into the race with characteristic verve. By challenging an incumbent president of his own party, Bobby Kennedy was taking an enormous risk. He might be destroying his entire career. But at least he was being true to himself and his convictions. At this moment, he could conceive only of victory.

Bobby hoped that McCarthy would withdraw in his favor, but McCarthy had no intention of withdrawing. He and his student activists and young idealists had worked feverishly hard to get this far. They weren't going to give up now.

On March 16, 1968, Bobby announced his candidacy for president of the United States in the Senate Caucus Room, where eight years earlier his brother had announced his bid for the presidency. On the same day, in the village of My Lai, nine thousand miles away, American soldiers, ordered by Lieutenant William Calley, killed unarmed men, women, and children and buried them in mass graves. The crime would shatter America's conscience.

Nine of Bobby's ten children heard their father's declaration: "I do not run for the presidency merely to oppose any man, but to propose new policies." He immediately tried to answer critics who would say he was running as a vendetta against LBJ.

Kennedy continued, "I run because I am convinced that this country is on a perilous course . . . I run to seek new policies—policies to end the bloodshed in Vietnam and in our cities, policies to close the gap that now exists between black and white, rich and poor, young and old . . . I run for the presidency because I want the Democratic Party and the United States of America to stand for hope, instead of despair, for the reconciliation of men instead of the growing risk of world war."[4]

In his rocking chair in the Oval Office, Lyndon Johnson looked out over the South Lawn and commented, "Bobby Kennedy has been a candidate since the first day I sat here."[5]

McCarthy supporters were outraged. They claimed that Kennedy was motivated only by power, that McCarthy had done the hard work of challenging Johnson. Few knew the treacherous inner tumult that Bobby had endured in mastering his fear to run. Few knew that his nephew George Skakel Jr. had been killed in Vietnam.

To stave off criticism from the McCarthy camp, Arthur Schlesinger, one of Bobby's advisers, recommended that he throw his support behind McCarthy and then later on the floor of the convention offer himself as a compromise candidate. But Bobby refused such a road. "Making speeches for him while I'm secretly trying to get delegates for myself—that's ruthless," he said. Besides, he didn't believe in McCarthy. "What has McCarthy ever done for the ghettos or the poor?" he asked.

In a televised speech on the final day of a cruel month of war and racial divisions, a heavyhearted Lyndon Baines Johnson told the nation that except for a small area in Vietnam, U.S. bombing would stop. He called for peace talks. He ended his speech with an announcement that shocked the nation: "I shall not seek, and I will not accept, the nomination of my party for another term as your president."

Bobby, too, was surprised. "I don't know quite what to say," he said to the press as he embarked on a whirlwind campaign.

If March was cruel, April would be crueler. On April 4, 1968, while Bobby was campaigning in Indiana, Dr. Martin Luther King Jr. was at the Lorraine Motel in Memphis, Tennessee, working out details for a nonviolent march on the streets of Memphis. King was scheduled to lead the peaceful event to support garbage collectors in their strike for higher wages. He was uneasy because his last march in Memphis had erupted in violence.

As King stood on the balcony outside his room, the sound of a gunshot cracked through the air. The Reverend Ralph Abernathy rushed to his friend's side, but already King was unconscious. He died of a gunshot wound in the neck.

When Bobby heard the news of Martin Luther King's assassination, he fell back as though he had been physically assaulted, and he wept. Bobby's staff worried that it was too dangerous for him to attend a scheduled rally in an Indianapolis ghetto.

"Cancel your speech," the Indianapolis police chief warned. "Nobody knows what's going to happen tonight."[6] But Bobby insisted on going. He told the crowd of one thousand people the news that they had not yet heard. Bobby's leadership was never more evident. He demonstrated ability to perform under pressure, and his courage and fearlessness were apparent as America erupted like a powder keg.

"For those of you who are black and are tempted to be filled with hatred and distrust at the injustice of such an act, against all white people, I can only say that I feel in my own heart the same kind of feeling. I had a member of my family killed, but he was killed by a white man. But we have to make an effort in the United States, we have to make an effort to understand, to go beyond these rather difficult times." To the silent, stunned, grieving crowd in Indianapolis's most impoverished neighborhood, Bobby revealed the depth of his own hurt about the murder of his brother Jack. It was the first time he had mentioned his brother's assassination in public.

Bobby quoted Aeschylus: " 'In our sleep, pain which cannot forget falls drop by drop upon the heart until, in our own despair, against our will, comes wisdom through the awful grace of God.' "

Comforted by the playwright's words, Bobby wanted to comfort others. Through suffering and grief, Aeschylus said, wisdom would be gained. Although the price was too great, the pain unbearable, suffering would bring wisdom.

"What we need in the United States is not division; what we need in the United States is not hatred; what we need in the United States is not violence or lawlessness, but love and wisdom, and compassion toward one another, and a feeling of justice toward those who still suffer within our country, whether they be white or they be black."

Bobby held up the words *love, wisdom, compassion,* and *justice* as vital to our survival as a nation.

Later that evening, Bobby placed a phone call to Coretta Scott King, widow of the minister. His staff arranged for a charter plane to return Martin Luther King's body to Atlanta, the place of his birth.

The slain leader was carried on a mule-drawn farm wagon through the streets of Atlanta as thousands mourned. And in the wake of the tragedy, riots and looting erupted in cities across the nation. People took to the streets, overturning cars, burning stores, and throwing rocks.

The following day in Cleveland, Bobby gave perhaps the most eloquent speech of his life. "Why? What has violence ever accomplished? What has it ever created? No martyr's cause has ever been stilled by his assassin's bullet. No wrongs have ever been righted by riots and civil disorders. A sniper is only a coward, not a hero, and an uncontrolled, uncontrollable mob is only the voice of madness, not the voice of the people.

"Whenever any American's life is taken by another American unnecessarily—whether it is done in the name of the law or in the defiance of law, by one man or a gang, in cold blood or in passion, in an attack of violence or in response to violence—whenever we tear at the fabric of life which another man has painfully and clumsily woven for himself and his children, the whole nation is degraded . . ."

Bobby had been challenged and galvanized by the poor and the downtrodden, and tormented by the plight of outcasts from privilege, but after Martin Luther King's death, he began to realize—and many people, too, realized—that he was the only political leader in America to whom the poor, both black and white, listened with respect. Bobby attributed many of America's problems primarily to poverty, and the poor gravitated toward him in even greater numbers. To a group of economically privileged individuals at the Indiana University Medical Center, Bobby said, "It's the poor who carry the major burden of the struggle in Vietnam. You sit here as white medical students, while black people carry the burden of fighting in Vietnam . . ."

There was a great deal of truth in his statement. A few days later, Bobby challenged another group of privileged people: "How many of you spend time over the summer, or on vacations, working in a black ghetto, or in eastern Kentucky, or on Indian reservations? Instead of asking what the federal government is doing about starving children, I say what is your

After riots in Washington, D.C., Bobby talks with a group of children.
MAGNUM

responsibility, what are you going to do about it? I think you people should organize yourselves right here, and try to do something about it."

He quoted Albert Camus, the French writer: " 'Perhaps we cannot prevent this world from being a world in which children are tortured. But we can reduce the number of tortured children.' "

Bobby preached compassion, but at times he generated viciousness and hate. "I don't understand it," Kennedy said. "I see people out there call me names, and say they want to actually hit me, and I just don't know what to say about it. The other day some fellow grabbed my hand in a motorcade and tried to squeeze it with all his might . . . Another person showed up at a lot of different places holding up a sign that just said 'YOU PUNK.' "[7]

Ethel was becoming alarmed by the large amount of hate mail Bobby's campaign was generating. Still she kept pace with him, often campaigning sixteen hours a day.

He plunged into crowds on the campaign trail in Indiana at a fever pitch. His hands became swollen and bruised from all the handshaking he had done. He was totally exhausted. One observer noted that he "looked like a fighter at the end of fifteen savage rounds."

Bobby won the Indiana primary. "I really have a chance now," he said, "just a chance, to organize a new coalition of Negroes, and working-class white people, against the union and party establishments."[8]

Inspired by the victory, Bobby seemed less tense, more his own person. He became even more deeply concerned with the lives of poor blacks and whites. He swept the Nebraska primary with 51.5 percent of the vote.

But in Oregon things went awry. His Oregon staff was persevering but small. At Kennedy headquarters in downtown Portland, there were only two desks and three workers. "There's nothing for me to get hold of," he said. Employment was high, and Bobby thought the people of the state were therefore not consumed by the burning issues of the day. His words seemed to fall on deaf ears.

There were light moments. At one rally, Bobby noticed a child holding out a box of chocolate-covered cherries. He took one and then offered the boy one, and the two new friends munched cheerfully.

Nevertheless, Oregon was Bobby Kennedy's first defeat. Eugene McCarthy won 44.7 percent of the vote in Oregon, Kennedy 38.8 percent.

Kennedy was good-natured about the loss. "I'm sorry I let you down," he said to David Borden, his lead student organizer in Oregon. Bobby was the first Kennedy to lose an election after twenty-seven consecutive victories. His defeat made him more human, more vulnerable, an underdog not only to himself but to others.

Bobby discovered that the fear of losing that had kept him out of the campaign was greater than the actual loss. "I can accept the fact that I may not be nominated now. If that happens, I will just go back to the Senate, and say what I believe, and not try again in '72. Somebody has to speak up for the Negroes, and Indians, and Mexicans, and poor whites. Maybe that's what I do best. Maybe my personality just isn't built for this . . . The issues are more important than me now." American cities were becoming armed camps and he intended to do something about it.

He received a rip-roaring welcome in Los Angeles, California. Unruly fans almost yanked Bobby out of his car.

In a televised debate with Eugene McCarthy, Bobby held his own, and in so doing broke McCarthy's momentum. But the frantic pace of the campaign had frazzled Bobby and brought him close to collapse.

On Monday, June 3, the final day of the campaign, Bobby's motorcade slithered through San Francisco's Chinatown. Five cracking explosions took place, and then five more, frightening people, reminding them of Dallas. Ethel crouched on the floor of the car. Bobby continued to shake hands and wave at the crowds, refusing to give way to fear. It was discovered that the explosions were caused by firecrackers.

He spent Tuesday, June 4, at Malibu, relaxing and swimming with Ethel and six of their children. The afternoon turned ugly when Bobby caught sight of his son David flailing in deep water. For frightening moments, David was caught in a powerful undertow. Bobby swam vigorously toward the boy and, against the surging tide, brought him back to shore.

In the early evening, the Kennedys arrived at their suite at the Ambassador Hotel in Los Angeles. As the results came pouring in, the atmosphere on the fifth floor became jubilant. Bobby had scored a sure victory in the California primary.

Bobby's campaign workers in the Ambassador's Embassy Ballroom sang, "This land is your land, this land is my land" and chanted, "We want Kennedy" and "We want Chavez." Bobby hoped that Chavez would join him on the platform. As Bobby made his way downstairs to claim his victory, he said to Kenny O'Donnell, "You know, Kenny. I feel now for the first time that I've shaken off the shadow of my brother. I feel I made it on my own."[9]

He gave a rousing victory statement. As he left the ballroom through the hotel kitchen, a shot rang out that brought Bobby to the floor.

The gunman had propped his elbow on a serving counter and fired at Bobby with an eight-shot revolver, a .22-caliber "long rifle." Bobby was no more than four feet away, walking toward the pressroom in a crowd of aides, supporters, and newspeople.

Olympic champion Rafer Johnson and L.A. Rams football lineman Roosevelt Grier grappled with the assailant, who kept pumping bullets. Five other people were wounded. Finally, the tiny, lithe gunman was over-powered. As Bobby lay dying, he whispered, "Is everybody okay?"[10]

David Kennedy, alone in his hotel bedroom, was the only Kennedy child to see television coverage of the murder. He heard the gunshots, the screams. On the television screen, he saw his father lying prostrate on the concrete floor.

A priest placed a rosary in the stricken candidate's hand. The priest was pushed aside as someone cried, "He doesn't need a priest, for God's sake, he needs a doctor!"

Ethel knelt over Bobby. Someone had grabbed ice from a large ice-making machine and placed an ice pack on his bleeding head. On the wall near the machine was a poster with the words "THE ONCE AND FUTURE KING" emblazoned across it.

Bobby was rushed to Central Receiving Hospital and then to Good Samaritan Hospital for surgery, Ethel by his side. At 2:00 A.M., over twenty-five hours after he had been shot, Frank Mankiewicz, Bobby's press secretary, his face contorted by grief, said: "I have a short announcement to read, which I will read at this time. Senator Robert Francis Kennedy died at 1:44 A.M. today, June 6, 1968. With Senator Kennedy at the time of his death were his wife, Ethel; his sisters, Mrs. Stephen Smith and Patricia Lawford; brother-in-law Stephen Smith; and Mrs. John F. Kennedy. He was forty-two years old." Teddy, too, was at his side.

The man seized at the Ambassador Hotel was Sirhan Bishara Sirhan, twenty-four years old. He was a Jordanian born in Jerusalem and had lived in Los Angeles for over ten years. He said that he hated Bobby because of his support for Israel in its conflict with the Arabs. But it clearly went beyond his animosity or one cause. Sirhan held an even greater rage that the American dream of wealth and power seemed totally beyond his grasp.

Bobby's closed mahogany casket was placed on the altar at New York's St. Patrick's Cathedral, where thousands of people paid their respects. In an incredible outpouring of grief, they bid farewell.

Bobby's children assisted in the solemn requiem mass; they and their young cousins served as acolytes. They carried the bread, the wine, and the sacred vessels.

A twenty-one-car railroad train carried the senator and his family and friends 226 miles south to the nation's capital. The train whistle—usually a cheerful, triumphant blast—took on a soulful, melancholy sound. As the train inched its way toward Washington, thousands along the route waved good-bye, many in tears.

The sun was intolerably hot and stifling. Some people threw flowers at the car carrying Bobby's flag-covered coffin. Many stood on track platforms; others on overpasses and rooftops. Some placed baseball caps over their hearts in final salute. High school bands rang out with "America." In Baltimore, grieving black mourners joined hands and sang "The Battle Hymn of the Republic."

Fifteen-year-old Joseph Kennedy Jr., the oldest Kennedy son, walked through each train car, introducing himself and thanking people for joining the family. Ethel followed close on his heels.

At 11:00 P.M., Bobby was placed to rest near the grave of his brother in Arlington National Cemetery. The site was just below the Lee-Custis Mansion and the eternal flame marking John F. Kennedy's grave. In final tribute, the Harvard University band played "America the Beautiful."

The words of Teddy Kennedy, spoken earlier in the day, echoed in the hearts of mourners. His voice cracked as he said, "My brother need not be

Robert Kennedy's funeral train drew thousands of mourners on its way to Washington, D.C.
AP/WIDE WORLD PHOTOS

idealized, or enlarged in death beyond what he was in life to be remembered simply as a good and decent man, who saw wrong and tried to right it, saw suffering and tried to heal it, saw war and tried to stop it." He concluded with lines from George Bernard Shaw that Bobby often quoted: "Some men see things as they are and say 'Why?' I dream things that never were and say 'Why not?' "

Epilogue

The years after Robert Kennedy's untimely death were a dark and turbulent time in the United States. In August, the Democratic Party held its national convention in Chicago. Outside the convention, three thousand antiwar demonstrators were turned back by tear gas and mace. Amidst the chaos, the Democrats nominated Vice President Hubert Humphrey as their candidate for president.

But the Democrats were badly divided by the events of the spring. Lyndon Johnson was continuing the war in Vietnam, and the deaths of Martin Luther King Jr. and Robert Kennedy shattered the dreams of Americans young and old who had hoped to see the country move away from violence and despair. In November 1968, Republican Richard Nixon, who had lost the 1960 election to John F. Kennedy, edged out Hubert Humphrey to become president of the United States.

Nixon's presidency ushered in an era of disillusionment, cynicism, and contempt for political institutions and leaders. It took more than five years of defeats on the battlefield and domestic protest before the United States pulled its troops out of Vietnam. And by that time, Nixon had disgraced the presidency with a series of scandals called Watergate.

It could have been different. No one can say for sure whether Robert Kennedy could have captured the Democratic nomination in 1968, much less won the general election in the fall. But one thing is certain: The country sorely missed his leadership and his idealism.

His life, his words, his actions, however, have continued to ripple through American history. Several of his children and nieces and nephews entered political life. His oldest son, Joe, was elected congressman from Massachusetts to the U.S. House of Representatives. His daughter Kathleen K. Townsend served as Maryland's lieutenant governor. His daughter Kerry Kennedy Cuomo became head of the Robert F. Kennedy Memorial Center for Human Rights. His brother Senator Edward M. Kennedy was elected in 1994 to a rare seventh term in the U.S. Senate.

One of Bobby's most impressive qualities was his capacity for growth. Early in his life, he saw things in terms of the good guys and the bad guys. Later, he became less certain, less self-righteous, and far more comfortable asking questions than giving answers. "I hope I've changed," he said. "I hope I've grown. I hope I have more understanding, more comprehension, and more compassion."[1]

Bobby was gifted with an intuitive feel for the underdog and an ability to put himself in another person's shoes. As he grew older, this unqualified empathy deepened and matured. "I think Bobby knows precisely what it feels like to be a very old woman," one person observed.[2]

This empathy, this ability to see through the eyes of another person, caused him to feel an intense sense of responsibility for others and a residual sadness. His conscience was highly developed, and the great social and moral issues of his time weighed heavily on him. He had difficulty distancing himself from problems, because he saw them from within.

He championed young people, but he also championed youth as a quality of the imagination. He was a Democrat but practiced a new kind of politics that transcended party lines and protocol—the politics of humanity. In his thinking he was prophetic. He grew less accepting of complacency on the part of the individual. "America can do better," he said.

"I'm impatient," he once said. "I would hope everybody would be impatient because you have only one time around. I think of all of the problems here on earth to which you must make a contribution of some kind."[3] Bobby Kennedy believed in the capacity of each person to feel life deeply and profoundly, in the right of each person to fulfill his potential, and in the obligation of each person to stand up and be counted.

Afterword

In writing the biography, we attempted to capture the infinite fragments of Bobby Kennedy's life as a brother, father, and political figure: his struggle growing up in a competitive family, his ardent efforts to live up to his father's expectations, and his commitment to the disinherited. We wanted to bring to life the idealist, the rebel, the private and public person.

Our work as directors of research for the film documentaries *Bobby Kennedy: In His Own Words* (HBO 1990) and *JFK: In His Own Words* (HBO 1988) contributed enormously to our portrait of Robert F. Kennedy. For more than three years at the John Fitzgerald Kennedy Library in Boston, we listened to recordings of extensive interviews with Bobby Kennedy, including interruptions by children, barking dogs, ringing telephones. We made use of the library's vast store of photographs, newspaper clippings, and films, including Kennedy family home movies. We witnessed Bobby on the campaign stump, in poverty pockets and ghetto streets, romping with his children at Hickory Hill. Actual film footage and recordings revealed Bobby confronting Jimmy Hoffa and Governor Ross Barnett, as well as climbing Mount Kennedy, skiing, ice-skating, playing touch football.

We are grateful to Peter Kunhardt, executive producer of the film documentaries, for inviting us to enter the world of the Kennedys. We would like to thank the tireless staff of the JFK Library; in particular, Allan Goodrich, audiovisual archivist, for assisting us in our research; and Sheldon Stern, historian, for reading the manuscript.

We are indebted to Bobby Kennedy's childhood friend David Hackett for his willingness to be interviewed and to Bobby's son Michael Kennedy for permitting us access to restricted family photographs

A special thanks, too, to our respective institutions, Brandeis University and the Newton Public Schools, and to Irwin Blumer, Superintendent; Judy Malone-Neville, principal; and staff members at the Charles E. Brown Middle School for their interest and affirmation.

We would also like to acknowledge family and friends for their support and encouragement: Jennie Alexander, Bill and Sophia Harrison, Kay and Glenn Groves, Lolly and Herb Selenkow, Vas and Ted Vrettos, Ethel and Paul Heins, Diane Carmody Wynne, Georgia L. Bartlett, Jeff Synder, and Olga Anastasia Pelensky.

To Maggie Stern Terris, much appreciation for her patience and her thoughtful, discerning reading of the manuscript.

During the challenging work of writing the biography, Virginia Buckley, our editor, contributed advice, insight, and encouragement. Her perceptions and recollections of the life and times of Bobby Kennedy were invaluable.

Endnotes

Chapter One

1 All chapter epigraphs are from Alfred, Lord Tennyson's poem "Ulysses," a poem of quest that held a special meaning for Robert Kennedy. The title of his 1967 book, *To Seek a Newer World,* is taken from this poem.

2 Burton Hersh, *The Education of Edward Kennedy: A Family Biography.* (New York: William Morrow, 1972), p. 20.

3 Clem Norton, *Oral History Interview.* (JFK Oral History Project), p. 20.

4 Arthur Schlesinger Jr., *Robert Kennedy and His Times.* (New York: Ballantine, 1985), p. 15.

5 Doris Kearns Goodwin, *The Fitzgeralds and the Kennedys: An American Saga.* (New York: Simon & Schuster, 1987), p. 367.

6 Jay Jacobs, ed., *RFK: His Life and Death.* (New York: Dell Publishing Co., Inc., 1968), p. 37.

7 Schlesinger, op. cit., p. 15.

8 Goodwin, op. cit., pp. 362–63.

9 Gail Cameron, *Rose: A Biography of Rose Fitzgerald Kennedy.* (New York: G. P. Putnam's Sons, 1971), p. 107.

10 Schlesinger, op. cit., p. 28.

11 Cameron, op. cit., p. 127.

12 Lester David and Irene David, *Bobby Kennedy: The Making of a Folk Hero.* (New York: Dodd, Mead & Company, 1986), p. 23.

13 Ibid., p. 28.

14 David Hackett, *Oral History Interview.* (RFK Oral History Project, July 22, 1970), p. 6.

15 David and David, op. cit., p. 30.

16 Sam Adams, *Oral History Interview.* (RFK Oral History Project), p. 6.

17 David and David, op. cit., p. 53.

18 Goodwin, op. cit., p. 761.

19 Robert E. Thompson and Hortense Myers, *Robert F. Kennedy: The Brother Within.* (New York: The Macmillan Company, 1962), p. 78.

Chapter Two

1 Kenneth P. O'Donnell and David F. Powers, *Johnny We Hardly Knew Ye: Memories of John Fitzgerald Kennedy.* (Boston: Little, Brown, 1972), p. 87.

2 George Plimpton, ed. *American Journey: The Times of Robert Kennedy.* Interviews by Jean Stein. (New York: Harcourt, 1960), p. 45.

3 Schlesinger, op. cit., p. 113.

4 Ibid., p. 173.

5 Ibid., p. 108.

6 Plimpton, op. cit., p. 55.

7 Robert F. Kennedy, *The Enemy Within* (New York, Harper and Brothers, 1960), pp. 40–43.

8 Schlesinger, op. cit., p. 153.

9 Ibid., p. 154.

10 Kennedy, op. cit., p. 56.

Chapter Three

1 Theodore White, *The Making of the President 1960* (New York: Atheneum, 1961), p. 383.

2 Schlesinger, op. cit., p. 214.

3 Ibid., pp. 246–47; John Siegenthaler, *Oral History Interview.* (RFK Oral History Project), vol. 3, p. 305.

4 Jacobs, op. cit., p. 83.

5 Schlesinger, op. cit., p. 247.

6 Siegenthaler, op. cit., vol. 3, p. 308.

7 Schlesinger, op. cit., pp. 249–50; Siegenthaler, op. cit., vol. 3, pp. 322–23.

8 David and David, op. cit., p. 130.

9 Schlesinger, op. cit., p. 276.

10 David and David, op. cit. pp. 132–33.

11 Plimpton, op. cit., p. 166.

12 Warren Rogers, *When I Think of Bobby: A Personal Memoir of the Kennedy Years.* (New York: HarperCollins, 1993), p. 89; Theodore C. Sorensen, *The Kennedy Legacy.* (New York: Macmillan, 1969), p. 23.

Chapter Four

1 Edwin O. Guthman, *We Band of Brothers.* (New York: Harper & Row, 1971), pp. 226–27.
2 *Newsweek,* June 17, 1968, p. 38.
3 Edwin O. Guthman and C. Richard Allen, *RFK: Collected Speeches* (New York: Viking, 1993), p. 51.
4 Plimpton, op. cit., p. 95; Schlesinger, op.cit., p. 296.
5 Ibid., p. 303.
6 Guthman, op. cit. pp. 228–29.
7 Schlesinger, op. cit. pp. 318–19.
8 Stein and Plimpton, op. cit., p. 118.
9 Ibid., pp. 119–22.

Chapter Five

1 Schlesinger, op. cit., p. 673; David and David, op.cit. pp. 150–51.
2 Schlesinger, op. cit., p. 658.
3 Manchester, p. 237.
4 Goodwin, op. cit., p. 41.
5 Schlesinger, op. cit., p. 718.
6 David and David, op. cit., p. 309.
7 James Whitaker, *Oral History Interview.* (RFK Oral History Project), p. 1.
8 Schlesinger, op. cit., p. 875.
9 Goodwin, op. cit., pp. 252–53.
10 Jules Witcover, *85 Days: The Last Campaign of Robert Kennedy.* (New York: G. P. Putnam's Sons, 1969), p. 19.
11 Penn Kimball, *Bobby Kennedy and the New Politics.* (New Jersey: Prentice Hall, 1978), p. 128.
12 Newfield, op. cit., p. 227.
13 Ibid., p. 228.
14 *Newsweek,* March 25, 1968.

Chapter Six

1 Newfield, op. cit., p. 227.
2 Ibid., p. 228.
3 Ibid., p. 240.
4 *Newsweek*, March 25, 1968.
5 *Time*, March 22, 1968, p. 17.
6 David and David, op. cit., p. 305.
7 Newfield, op. cit., p. 292.
8 Ibid., p. 302.
9 David and David, op. cit., p. 316.
10 *Newsweek*, May 31, 1993.

Epilogue

1 Peter Kunhardt, prod., *Bobby Kennedy: In His Own Words* (Home Box Office, 1990).
2 Newfield, op. cit., p. 38.
3 *Bobby Kennedy: In His Own Words*

Sources of Information

Several books shed light on Bobby Kennedy's life and times, including two first-rate biographies, Arthur M. Schlesinger Jr.'s *Robert Kennedy and His Times*, a compelling portrayal of Bobby and the turbulent era in which he lived; and Jack Newfield's *Robert Kennedy: A Memoir*, a passionate rendering of Bobby's life. Edwin O. Guthman and C. Richard Allen's *RFK: Collected Speeches*, a selection of evocative public statements by Bobby Kennedy coupled with historical and personal commentary, is a more recent and welcome addition to Bobby Kennedy scholarship.

Edwin O. Guthman's *We Band of Brothers* and David Halberstam's *The Unfinished Odyssey of Robert Kennedy* are among the many books that were published in the late sixties and early seventies, just after Bobby's assassination. *RFK: His Life and Death* (by the editors of American Heritage, narrative written by Jay Jacobs) is noteworthy for its brevity and insight. Stirring reminiscences by individuals aboard Bobby's funeral train and along the train route are juxtaposed with lively interviews disclosing Bobby's life story in *American Journey: The Times of Robert Kennedy*, edited by George Plimpton with interviews by Jean Stein.

Other books for the general reader were published in the 1980s, including Lester and Irene David's spirited and informative *Bobby Kennedy: The Making of a Folk Hero*; Richard N. Goodwin's *Remembering America*, an engrossing odyssey of the 1960s; and Doris Kearns Goodwin's *The Fitzgeralds and the Kennedys: An American Saga*, the story of three generations of Fitzgeralds and Kennedys. Harvey Rachlin provides a useful almanac of charts, photographs, and timelines in *The Kennedys: A Chronological History, 1823–Present*.

Books that explore Kennedy family controversy include *R.F.K.: The Man Who Would Be President* by Ralph de Toledano; *The Kennedy Neurosis: A Psychological Portrait of an American Dynasty,* by Nancy Gager Clinch; and most recently, Jerry Oppenheimer's *The Other Mrs. Kennedy: Ethel Skakel Kennedy: An American Drama of Power, Privilege, and Politics.*

Family and friends, including schoolmates David Hackett and Samuel Adams and the Kennedy family nurse, Luella R. Hennessey, share personal recollections in *That Shining Hour,* edited by Bobby's sister Patricia Kennedy Lawford and privately published by the Kennedy family. Rose Fitzgerald Kennedy's autobiography *Times to Remember* reveals intimate vignettes about the family. Heartfelt commentary by Native Americans, farmworkers, journalists—admirers, but not all personal friends—is included in *An Honorable Profession: A Tribute to Robert F. Kennedy.* The book contains an introduction by Bobby's daughter Kerry Kennedy Cuomo and is edited by Pierre Salinger, Edwin O. Guthman, Frank Mankiewicz, and John Siegenthaler.

Bobby's own books also contribute to the reader's perception of the man: *The Enemy Within* (1960), *Just Friends and Brave Enemies* (1962), *The Pursuit of Justice* (1964), *To Seek a Newer World* (1967), and *Thirteen Days: A Memoir of the Cuban Missile Crisis* (1969). In addition, *Robert Kennedy In His Own Words: The Unpublished Recollections of the Kennedy Years,* edited by Edwin O. Guthman and Jeffrey Shulman, contains interviews conducted with Bobby Kennedy. Drawn from the oral history collection of the JFK Library, the interviews were conducted before Bobby was even forty years old and bring to the fore evidence that would have vanished with his death.

In addition to books, there exists an enormous body of newspaper and magazine articles ranging from such items as "Young Man with Tough Questions" in *Life* magazine to "The Real Robert F. Kennedy" in *Ladies' Home Journal.* Audiotapes and films of Bobby's tours of Europe, Asia, South America, and Africa; radio and television interviews, for example, his appearance on the David Frost television show in 1968, television advertisements, and home movies are all grist for the biographer and historian.

The JFK Library in Boston remains the best single source of information on the life of Bobby Kennedy, because it gathers under its roof both a museum that exhibits documents and memorabilia and contains an extensive print and audiovisual library.

Selected Bibliography

David, Lester, and Irene David. *Bobby Kennedy: The Making of a Folk Hero.* New York: Dodd, Mead & Company, 1986.

Goodwin, Doris Kearns. *The Fitzgeralds and the Kennedys: An American Saga.* New York: Simon & Schuster, 1987.

———*Lyndon Johnson and the American Dream.* New York: St. Martin's Press, 1991.

Goodwin, Richard N. *Remembering America: A Voice from the Sixties.* Boston: Little, Brown, 1988.

Guthman, Edwin O. *We Band of Brothers.* New York: Harper & Row, 1971.

Guthman, Edwin O., and C. Richard Allen. *RFK: Collected Speeches.* New York: Viking, 1993.

Kennedy, Rose Fitzgerald. *Times to Remember.* New York: Doubleday, 1995.

Laing, Margaret. *The Next Kennedy.* New York: Coward-McCann, Inc., 1968.

Lawford, Patricia Kennedy, ed. *That Shining Hour.* Printed in the U.S. by Halliday Lithograph Corporation, Copyright Patricia Kennedy Lawford, 1969.

Newfield, Jack. *Robert Kennedy: A Memoir.* New York: Dutton, 1969, Bantam, 1970.

Plimpton, George, ed. *American Journey: The Times of Robert Kennedy.* Interviews by Jean Stein. New York: Harcourt, 1960.

Rachlin, Harvey. *The Kennedys: A Chronological History, 1823–Present.* New York: World Almanac, 1986.

Robert Kennedy in South Africa: A Souvenir Booklet of Senator Kennedy's 1966 Tour of South Africa. Compiled by *Daily Rand Mail,* 1966.

Salinger, Pierre, and Edwin O. Guthman, Frank Mankiewicz, and John Siegenthaler. *An Honorable Profession: A Tribute to Robert F. Kennedy.* Introduction by Kerry Kennedy Cuomo. New York: Main Street Books, Doubleday, 1993.

Schlesinger, Arthur M., Jr. *Robert Kennedy and His Times.* Boston: Houghton Mifflin, 1978, Ballantine, 1985.

Zinn, Howard. *A People's History of the United States.* New York: HarperCollins, 1990.

Chronology

NOVEMBER 20, 1925   Robert Kennedy is born at the family home at 51 Abbottsford Road in Brookline, Massachusetts. He is the seventh child of Rose (Fitzgerald) and Joseph P. Kennedy.

SEPTEMBER 1927   The Kennedy family—Joe Sr., Rose, Joe Jr., John, Rosemary, Kathleen, Eunice, Patricia, and Robert—moves to New York.

FEBRUARY 20, 1928   Bobby's sister Jean is born.

MARCH 4, 1929   Herbert Hoover takes the oath of office as president of the United States.

FEBRUARY 22, 1932   Bobby's brother Edward Moore, called "Teddy," is born.

MARCH 4, 1933   Franklin Delano Roosevelt is sworn in as the thirty-second president of the United States.

JANUARY 5, 1938   President Franklin Delano Roosevelt appoints Joseph P. Kennedy ambassador to Great Britain.

MARCH 9, 1938   Bobby, 12, leaves on board an ocean liner for England with his mother and four siblings: Kathleen, Patricia, Jean, and Edward.

SEPTEMBER 1, 1939   Germany invades Poland, marking the beginning of World War II.

SEPTEMBER 3, 1939   England enters the war, and shortly afterward Bobby and his family leave wartorn Europe by ship to return to America.

SEPTEMBER 19, 1939   Bobby, 13, enters eighth grade at St. Paul's School in Concord, New Hampshire.

OCTOBER 6, 1939   Bobby withdraws from St. Paul's School, and shortly afterward he enters eighth grade at Portsmouth Priory in Portsmouth, Rhode Island.

DECEMBER 7, 1941   Pearl Harbor, Hawaii, is attacked by the Japanese, and the following day the United States enters World War II.

SEPTEMBER 23, 1942   Bobby, 16, transfers to Milton Academy in Milton, Massachusetts, where he begins his junior year.

AUGUST 2, 1943   Lt. (jg) John F. Kennedy's PT-109, a patrol boat, carrying a crew of thirteen, is sunk by a Japanese destroyer in the South Pacific.

OCTOBER 5, 1943   Bobby, 17, enlists as a Seaman Apprentice in the United States Naval Reserve at the Naval Aviation Cadet Selection Board in Boston.

MARCH 1, 1944   Bobby, 18, reports to the Navy V-12 unit at Harvard University.

MAY 27, 1944   Bobby, 18, graduates from Milton Academy.

AUGUST 12, 1944   Lt. Joseph P. Kennedy Jr. is killed instantly when his PB-44 drone Liberator bomber explodes over the English Channel.

NOVEMBER 1, 1944   Bobby reports to Bates College in Lewiston, Maine, for training with the U.S. Navy.

NOVEMBER 6, 1944   Bobby enters his freshman year at Harvard University, although his college years are interrupted by the war.

APRIL 12, 1945   President Franklin Delano Roosevelt dies, and Harry S. Truman becomes president of the United States.

FEBRUARY 1, 1946   Bobby is assigned to active duty aboard the USS *Joseph P. Kennedy Jr.*, a destroyer named in honor of his war hero brother.

MAY 30, 1946   Bobby is discharged from active duty in the U.S. Navy.

NOVEMBER 5, 1946   John Kennedy is elected to the U.S. House of Representatives from Massachusetts. Bobby has campaigned for Jack in his first bid for political office.

MAY 13, 1948   Bobby's oldest sister, Kathleen Kennedy Cavendish, Lady Hartington, is killed in a plane crash in southern France.

JUNE 10, 1948   Bobby, 22, graduates from Harvard University. He becomes a correspondent for the *Boston Post* and is sent to Palestine to cover the Arab-Israeli conflict.

SEPTEMBER 16, 1948   Bobby enters the University of Virginia Law School.

JUNE 17, 1950   Bobby, 24, marries Ethel Skakel, 22, at St. Mary's Roman Catholic Church in Greenwich, Connecticut. His brother Jack is the best man. Bobby is the first Kennedy brother to marry.

JUNE 11, 1951   Bobby graduates from the University of Virginia Law School.

JULY 4, 1951   Kathleen Hartington Kennedy is born in Greenwich, Connecticut. Kathleen is Bobby and Ethel's first child and Rose and Joe Kennedy's first grandchild.

NOVEMBER 21, 1951   Bobby is admitted to the Massachusetts bar and is appointed an attorney adviser in the Criminal Division of the Department of Justice in Washington, D.C.

JUNE 6, 1952   Bobby resigns from his job as a government attorney to manage his brother's campaign for a seat in the U.S. Senate.

SEPTEMBER 24, 1952   Joseph Patrick II is born in Brighton, Massachusetts. Joseph is Bobby and Ethel's second child and first son.

NOVEMBER 4, 1952   John Fitzgerald Kennedy wins his election to the U.S. Senate, defeating three-term Republican Henry Cabot Lodge Jr. Republican candidate Dwight D. Eisenhower is elected president and Richard M. Nixon is elected vicepresident.

JANUARY 14, 1952   Bobby Kennedy, 26, is appointed assistant counsel to the Senate Permanent Subcommittee on Investigations headed by Senator Joseph McCarthy.

JULY 31, 1953   Bobby resigns his post as assistant counsel to McCarthy's investigations committee.

SEPTEMBER 12, 1953   Bobby serves as best man in his brother Jack's wedding to Jacqueline Lee Bouvier in Newport, Rhode Island.

JANUARY 17, 1954   Robert Francis Jr. is born in Washington, D.C. Robert is Bobby and Ethel's third child and second son.

FEBRUARY 16, 1954   Bobby is reappointed to the Senate Permanent Subcommittee on Investigations as chief counsel to the Democratic minority.

JANUARY 5, 1955   Bobby is appointed chief counsel and staff director of the Senate Permanent Subcommittee on Investigations.

JUNE 15, 1955   David Anthony is born in Washington, D.C. He is Bobby and Ethel's fourth child.

AUGUST 17, 1956   Jack Kennedy is defeated by Estes Kefauver in his bid for the Democratic Party's vice-presidential nomination.

SEPTEMBER 9, 1956   Mary Courtney is born in Boston, Massachusetts. She is Ethel and Bobby's second daughter and fifth child.

FEBRUARY 26, 1957   The Senate Select Committee on Improper Activities in the Labor or Management Field (popularly called the Rackets Committee) opens hearings in Washington, D.C. Robert F. Kennedy serves as chief counsel.

AUGUST 20–21, 1957   Bobby questions James R. Hoffa, leader in the International Brotherhood of Teamsters, at hearings of the Senate Rackets Committee.

FEBRUARY 27, 1958   Michael LeMoyne is born in Washington, D.C. Michael is Bobby and Ethel's sixth child.

SEPTEMBER 8, 1959   Mary Kerry is born in Washington, D.C. She is Bobby and Ethel's seventh child.

SEPTEMBER 10, 1959   Bobby resigns his position as chief counsel of the Rackets Committee to write a book on rackets investigations and to manage his brother's bid for the presidential nomination.

JANUARY 2, 1960   John F. Kennedy announces his candidacy for the presidency of the United States. Bobby works full-time during 1960 running his brother's campaign.

JULY 13, 1960   John F. Kennedy wins the Democratic Party's presidential nomination on the first ballot.

NOVEMBER 8, 1960   John F. Kennedy is elected president of the United States.

DECEMBER 16, 1960   Bobby is appointed attorney general by president-elect John F. Kennedy.

APRIL 17, 1961   Bay of Pigs invasion in which more than 1,200 anti-Castro Cuban exiles attempt to overthrow the government of Premier Fidel Castro

MAY 6, 1961 Bobby delivers the commencement address at the University of Georgia Law School.

MAY 20, 1961 Bobby orders 400 U.S. marshals into Montgomery, Alabama, to protect the Freedom Riders.

MAY 21, 1961 Martin Luther King Jr. calls Bobby Kennedy to alert him to the danger King and other blacks are facing at the First Baptist Church in Montgomery.

FEBRUARY 1, 1962 Bobby and Ethel begin a one-month goodwill tour of the Far East.

FEBRUARY 4, 1962 Leftist youths disrupt a talk by Bobby at Waseda University in Japan.

SEPTEMBER 29, 1962 Federal marshals are sent to Mississippi to ensure the attendance of a black veteran, James H. Meredith Jr., at the University of Mississippi.

OCTOBER 16–28, 1962 Cuban Missile Crisis

JANUARY 17, 1963 Before the Supreme Court, Bobby Kennedy argues against the legality of Georgia's county-unit system of voting.

MAY 2–3, 1963 Black schoolchildren march in Birmingham, Alabama.

JUNE 19, 1963 President John F. Kennedy sends a comprehensive civil rights bill to Congress.

JULY 4, 1963 Christopher George is born in Boston. He is Ethel and Bobby's eighth child.

JULY 25, 1963 A limited nuclear test–ban treaty is agreed on by the Soviet Union, Great Britain, and the United States.

AUGUST 28, 1963 Over 200,000 people gather at the Lincoln Memorial in the largest civil rights demonstration the nation has ever seen. Martin Luther King Jr. delivers his "I have a dream" speech.

NOVEMBER 22, 1963 President Kennedy is assassinated in Dallas, Texas.

DECEMBER 4, 1963 Bobby resumes his work as attorney general at the Justice Department.

MARCH 17, 1964   Bobby breaks ground in Scranton, Pennsylvania, for the first elementary school to be named for President Kennedy.

AUGUST 25, 1964   Bobby declares his candidacy for the Democratic nomination for U.S. senator from New York.

AUGUST 27, 1964   Bobby gives a brief speech honoring his brother Jack at the Democratic National Convention.

SEPTEMBER 1, 1964   Bobby wins the nomination for U.S. senator from New York on the first ballot.

OCTOBER 20, 1964   *The Pursuit of Justice,* a book by Bobby about his work as attorney general, is published by Harper & Row.

NOVEMBER 3, 1964   Bobby is elected U.S. senator from New York, defeating Republican candidate Kenneth B. Keating.

DECEMBER 4, 1964   *Rights for Americans: The Speeches of Robert F. Kennedy* is published by Bobbs-Merrill Company.

JANUARY 4, 1965   For the first time since 1800, two brothers are sworn in as United States senators: Bobby Kennedy from New York and Edward M. Kennedy from Massachusetts.

JANUARY 11, 1965   Matthew Maxwell Taylor is born in New York. He is Bobby and Ethel's ninth child.

MARCH 24, 1965   Bobby Kennedy becomes the first person to scale Mount Kennedy, named in memory of his brother Jack; Mount Kennedy in Canada is 13,880 feet high.

NOVEMBER 10, 1965–DECEMBER 1, 1965   Bobby makes an unofficial three-week fact-finding tour of Latin America.

JUNE 6, 1966   Bobby gives a speech to an audience of 16,000 at the University of Cape Town, South Africa, in which he condemns apartheid.

DECEMBER 9, 1966   Bobby announces a program to develop the Bedford-Stuyvesant community in Brooklyn.

MARCH 24, 1967   Douglas Harriman is born in Washington, D.C. He is Bobby and Ethel's tenth child.

APRIL 11, 1967 Bobby visits poor black communities in the Mississippi Delta.

MAY 17, 1967 Bobby Kennedy cosponsors a bill requiring cigarette manufacturers to advertise on cigarette packages the dangers of smoking.

NOVEMBER 24, 1967 *To Seek a Newer World,* a book of Robert Kennedy's speeches, is published by Doubleday and Company.

JANUARY 31, 1968 Bobby speaks out against the bombing of North Vietnam.

MARCH 7, 1968 Robert Kennedy condemns administration policy on the Vietnam War in a passionate speech before the U.S. Senate.

MARCH 10, 1968 Robert Kennedy joins Cesar Chavez in Delano, California, at a rally marking the end of Chavez's fast to protest treatment of migrant farmworkers.

MARCH 16, 1968 Bobby Kennedy announces his candidacy for president of the United States.

APRIL 4, 1968 Martin Luther King Jr. is assassinated in Memphis, Tennessee.

JUNE 5, 1968 Robert Kennedy is mortally wounded by a gunman at the Ambassador Hotel in Los Angeles, California.

JUNE 6, 1968 Robert Kennedy, 42 years old, dies at 1:44 a.m. of gunshot wounds.

DECEMBER 12, 1968 Rory Elizabeth Katherine Kennedy is born in Washington, D.C. Rory is Bobby and Ethel's eleventh child.

Index

Page numbers in *italics* refer to photographs.

About the Authors

BARBARA HARRISON teaches English at the Charles E. Brown Middle School in Newton, Massachusetts, and co-directs Children's Literature New England. With Daniel Terris, she is co-author of *A Twilight Struggle: The Life of John Fitzgerald Kennedy.* She lives in Cambridge, Massachusetts.

DANIEL TERRIS is executive director of the International Center for Ethics, Justice, and Public Life at Brandeis University, and he has served as president of the Foundation for Children's Books. He lives in Concord, Massachusetts, with his wife, Maggie, and his four sons, Ben, Eli, Theo, and Sam.

Harrison and Terris directed research for the award-winning HBO documentaries, *JFK: In His Own Words* and *Bobby Kennedy: In His Own Words.*

16.99 , 16.99

DATE			